MW00637254

AWAY
FROM
FREEDOM

The revolt of the college economists

VERVON ORVAL WATTS

The Ludwig von Mises Institute
Auburn, Alabama
2008

DR. ORVAL WATTS is an economist. Teaching is his career. He has taught economics to college students for seventeen years — at Harvard University, Clark University, Wellesley College, Antioch College, Carleton College, and Claremont Men's College.

He has taught economics to businessmen as economic consultant, lecturer and author. His twelve years in this work overlapped his college teaching somewhat and included positions as economist for the Los Angeles Chamber of Commerce and The Foundation for Economic Education. He is now serving as economic consultant for Freedom Clubs, Inc., as well as for several leading business concerns in Southern California.

He contributes to various magazines which concern themselves with public affairs; he is a columnist for *Christian Economics*. His books: *Why Are We So Prosperous?*, *Do We Want Free Enterprise?*

The Foundation for Social Research is an independent non-profit, non-political organization devoted to carrying on research projects in the social sciences.

FREEDOM CENTER BUILDING
1521 WILSHIRE BOULEVARD, LOS ANGELES 17, CALIFORNIA

Preface

V. Orval Watts, one of the leading free-market economists of the World War II and post-war eras, died on March 30 this year. When I first met him, in the winter of 1947, he was a leading economist at the Foundation for Economic Education (FEE), the only free-market organization and think-tank of that era. He was a pleasantly sardonic man in his late forties. Born in 1898 in Manitoba, Vernon Orval Willard Watts was graduated from the University of Manitoba in 1918, and went on to earn a master's and a doctor's degree in economics from Harvard University in its nobler, pre-Keynesian era.

After teaching economics at various colleges, Orval was hired by Leonard Read in 1939 to be the economist for the Los Angeles Chamber of Commerce, of which Leonard was executive director. Watts thereby became the first full-time economist to be employed by a chamber of commerce in the United States.

Leonard Read had built up the Los Angeles Chamber into the largest municipal business organization in the world, and Read himself had been converted to the libertarian, free-market creed by a remarkable constituent of the Chamber: William C.

Mullendore, head of the Southern California Edison Corporation.

During World War II, Read, assisted by Watts, lent his remarkable organizing talents to making the Los Angeles Chamber a beacon of freedom in an increasingly collectivist world. When Read took the bold step of moving to Irvington-on-Hudson in New York to set up FEE in 1946, he took Orval with him as his economic adviser.

During World War II, Orval published book *Do We Want Free Enterprise?* (1944). In his FEE years, he published several books, as well as writing numerous articles for free-market publications. His books included *Away From Freedom* (1952), a critique of Keynesianism; his pungent critique of unions, *Union Monopoly* (1954), and his perceptive attack on the United Nations, *United Nations: Planned Tyranny* (1955). He also served as economic counsel to Southern California Edison and several other companies in the Los Angeles area.

In 1963, at an age (65) where most men are thinking seriously of retirement, Orval resumed his teaching career, moving to the recently established Northwood University (then Northwood Institute), a free-market center of learning in Midland, Michigan.

Orval, bless him, served as director of economic education and chairman of the Division of Social Studies at Northwood for twenty-one years, until he retired in 1984 at the age of 86. While at Northwood, he published an excellent anthology of free market vs. government intervention articles, *Free Markets or Famine?* (1967), as well as his final book *Politics vs. Prosperity* (1976).

Orval Watts died in Palm Springs, California, this March, having just turned 95. He is survived by his wife Carolyn, a son, three daughters, nine grandchildren, and two great-grandchildren.

We can see in the present world how vitally important history is for the values and self-definition of a family, a movement, or a nation. As a result, history has become a veritable cockpit of contending factions. Any movement that has no sense of its own history, that fails to acknowledge its own leaders and heroes, is not going to amount to very much, nor does it deserve a better fate.

Murray N. Rothbard
July 1993

Foreword

Given one set of ideas, a man may starve himself to death or throw himself before a speeding train. Given other ideas, he may work from dawn to dusk for a pittance.

For man is a creature of ideas. "As he thinketh in his heart, so is he." What he does today depends on what he thought yesterday. What he may do tomorrow depends on what he thinks now and will think then. Soldiers fight the wars that make headlines, but back of the men of force are thinkers and talkers who tell them whom to fight and when.

Truth, therefore, is as necessary to human life as food and drink. Wrong ideas may be as deadly as any poison or virus. Right ideas mean health and progress.

Most Americans know this. They know that right thinking is essential for the good life they want their children to have. So they try to educate them in truth and right. They build temples of learning, hire much-schooled teachers, spend freely on "wholesome" entertainments, endow colleges, attend meetings, serve as trustees, scold their children, support alumni organizations—and hope!

It is with this costly effort in mind that I have written this booklet. I think I have something important to tell those who spend so much time and money on education about what they are getting for their many sacrifices.

In addition, every businessman and investor, every wage earner and salaried worker—in fact, everyone who plans for the future—will succeed or fail in his economic endeavors according as he knows what his fellow citizens may think and do in the future. What teachers tell their students is going to help determine future property values and tax rates, employment and wage levels, prices and interest rates, controls and subsidies.

And should not every educator or scientist, no matter what his field, be concerned about what his colleagues are doing? Will not the success of his own life's work depend much on the help he gets in discovering and disseminating truth in other fields?

In the following pages I try to show as simply as I can how the most popular writers of economics textbooks now treat the problems of government spending, taxes, and money. I give their arguments for higher taxes on the well-to-do, subsidies to non-producers, more government borrowing, and the inconvertible money that makes it all possible. I point out similarities between their theory and that of Karl Marx, the messiah of Communism. I try to show where the theory leads in the realm of private morals and personal conduct, as well as in government and politics; and I give reasons for thinking that it is reactionary and false.

In striving for brevity and clarity, however, I necessarily sacrifice much. I do not give a comprehensive survey of economics textbooks or of all the teachings of any textbook. My survey even of the one school of thought is only partial and incomplete. I cannot in this brief study give all the ramifications and criticisms of a theory that its advocates set forth in many volumes.

However, I do not think it necessary to pursue in all its details a theory that starts from wrong premises and ends with unworkable conclusions. The basic fallacies of it, I believe, are not hard to understand, and the menace of its conclusions is daily becoming more evident. If this is so, it is important that these elements of understanding be made readily available.

In my opinion, the new point of view, which its proponents call the "New Economics," or the "Keynesian Revolution," has done great harm to students whom I have seen fall victim to it.

Even now, I believe, it is destroying the foundations of our nation.

V. ORVAL WATTS
Altadena, California
January, 1952

TABLE OF CONTENTS

flation, not expansion, of credit; Credit currency may be preferred; In free markets, goods generate credit; The basic fallacy of Keynesian theory; Goods give value to goods; Credit vs. credit instruments; Goods pay for goods; Is saving dangerous? Savings increase demand for labor; Inventions increase profits and wages; When lower profits mean higher wages; Inflation robs producers and destroys credit; Government policies caused inflation, 1913-29; Corporations save in order to invest; "We planned it that way"; The growing appetite for inflation.

I. "The Keynesian Revolution"

UNTIL THE end of World War II, the most widely used economics textbooks in America were still in the classical tradition. They taught that free enterprise was a workable system. It had its faults, they said, such as inequalities and monopolies, but at least it gave us a maximum of individual opportunity and economic progress.

What the "new economists" propose

Now the most widely used textbooks present a very different view, one which the authors call the "new economics," or the "Keynesian revolution." This new set of doctrines purports to prove that free enterprise, in addition to other alleged faults, is "without a steering wheel or governor," inherently unstable and inefficient.

Because of this inherent and basic defect, the theory goes, a "mature" economy like that of the United States must suffer an intolerable degree of unemployment and unused capacity—unless government comes to the rescue.

Government is to effect this rescue by taking

charge of all incomes, savings, investment and spending. It is to exercise its control through taxation, subsidies, government ownership and executive orders. The aim is to regulate spending, saving, investment, prices and wages so that the flow of spending always equals the flow of goods, thus bringing about full employment and capacity production without *too much* inflation.

This government "management" is labelled a "compensatory fiscal and monetary policy."

A "managed economy" from now on

Of course, governments throughout the world are already following such a policy to a greater or less extent. But many persons, especially in the United States, hopefully believe that it is in some way connected with war or the threat of war. They are vaguely aware that some economists and politicians want to make it permanent and more complete. But they think that such "radicals" are in a minority. They expect more "conservative" leadership will eventually win out, put a stop to the present drift, and restore at least enough freedom of enterprise so that America may once again become a land of ever more abundant opportunity. Furthermore, they hope that this reversal of the trend will come about before any great disaster overtakes them.

What such optimists do not realize is that a revolution in economic thought now taking place in

American colleges and universities is rapidly making any reversal of the present trends increasingly difficult and improbable. Still less do these optimists realize that disaster may even now be overtaking them and multitudes of other individuals as they fall victims to the supposedly new economic thought and policy.

"Keynes . . . had the revelation"

Typical of this "new economics" is the book which has held first place in college adoptions since 1949: *Economics, An Introductory Analysis,* by Paul A. Samuelson, professor of economics at the Massachusetts Institute of Technology. Other textbook writers of the same school of thought are Lorie Tarshis, Seymour Harris, Theodore Morgan, Richard Ruggles, Lawrence R. Klein, J. A. Nordin and Virgil Salera.[1]

These authors and teachers, along with hundreds or thousands of their associates, are deliberately and systematically trying to bring about what they themselves call a revolution in the economics being taught to American college students.

According to a survey reported in the *American Economic Review* for December, 1950 (Supplement, Part 2), nearly 80 per cent of the college teachers questioned were then teaching economics from the point of view of the "new economics."

Until recently, the authors of this revolution did not hesitate to call themselves "Keynesians." Now,

3

most of them call their view the "national income approach," or "the national income determination-full employment approach." But, as Professor Harris, one of their number, says, it was Lord Keynes who "had the revelation." It was this English economist who revived and popularized the old pattern of thought which is the core of their system. "His disciples are now divided into groups," continues Harris, "each taking sustenance from the Keynesian larder. The struggle for the Apostolic Succession is on."[2]

"The reign of laissez faire has ended"

It was during the 1920s, in England, that "the revelation" came to this modern oracle, and perhaps one may better understand the message if he knows the circumstances which inspired it.

The problem which the economists of that country were debating was unemployment. From 1920 to 1937, except for one year, unemployment in England remained above 10 per cent of the labor force, a level equalled only twice before in the preceding 60 years.

Classical economists said that the causes of this chronic unemployment were interferences with free enterprise: heavy taxes and burdensome government restrictions; unemployment doles, which subsidized idleness; and trade union wage-kiting and restriction of output. The remedy, these economists argued, was to remove or reduce these burdens and restrictions.

4

The trade union leaders, of course, indignantly rejected this argument. So did the Fabian Socialists, who held many academic positions. However, the attack on the free-market theory of prosperity lacked academic prestige until John Maynard Keynes, a tutor at the University of Cambridge, joined in.

The inflation cure for unemployment

At first Keynes argued that cutting wages was the wrong remedy for unemployment in depressions because of "wage rigidities" arising from trade unionism and social security. In other words, at lower wages more jobs might be open but the unions and the doles would keep workers from taking them. Keynes said it would take years of mass unemployment to induce workers to accept lower wage rates, and that was too high a price to pay for free markets. The reign of *laissez faire* in England had ended, he said, and economists might as well stop pleading for it.

The only feasible remedy for the unemployment, in Keynes's opinion, was to raise the price level so that employers could pay the wages demanded by the unions. To this end, he urged that the government and the Bank of England reduce interest rates and encourage an expansion of bank credit, even if this meant devaluing the currency in terms of gold.

The classicists, or free-enterprise economists, replied that the easy-money policy advocated by

Keynes would be dishonest and dangerous. It would mean cutting the purchasing power of wages, and it would work only if the workers did not find out what was going on. If or when they learned the truth, they would demand wage increases to match the rise in living costs. This would nullify any possible benefits of inflation in reducing unemployment. They charged further that the devaluation of the pound or continued inconvertibility which Keynes advocated would violate a trust and endanger the business of England's bankers, who financed most of the world's international trade.

Why Keynes attacked thrift

In short, Keynes's critics accused him of using the argument of political expediency to justify a bad economic policy.

In reply, Keynes tried to show that wage-maintenance and currency inflation are good economics as well as good politics, as long as there is less than "full employment." For this purpose, he had to find some cause for chronic, large-scale unemployment other than high wage rates, high taxes, and the dole. He professed to find it in hoarded (uninvested) savings. Consequently, as Harris says, he began an "all-out attack on thriftiness."[3]

Economists used to teach that individuals save mainly in order to invest or to spend later. They pointed out that most of the savings are deposited in banks, which lend them to businessmen and other producers. These borrowers spend ("invest") the money for goods and services used in production. This keeps the money circulating and maintains the demand for labor. A rise in the supply of savings leads to a fall in the rate of interest, and this decline in interest rates stimulates borrowing and investment. An increase in investment opportunities leads to a rise in interest rates, which in turn encourages saving. Thus the supply of savings in free markets tends to equal the demand for loans to be used in financing production.

". . . the system is in the lap of the gods"

Keynes and his disciples repudiate this line of reasoning. They deny that individuals, if left free to choose, adjust the flow of savings to the rate of investment or the rate of investment to the flow of savings. Says Samuelson, author of the best seller among college textbooks in economics: "Whatever the individual's motivation to save, it has little directly to do with investment or investment opportunities . . . saving and investing are done by different individuals and for largely independent reasons."[4]

It is only an accident, he asserts, if investments at any time equal the sums which individuals want to put aside as savings. Consequently, if individuals are left free to save as much as they wish, the result may be chronic depression and large-scale unemployment. Investors, explorers, and promoters may fail to open up sufficient new investment opportunities to induce businessmen to borrow the savings and put them to work, or population may not grow fast enough to provide markets for the products of the new machines in which businessmen invest. Or, the opposite may happen. Investment opportunities may increase faster than savings. If free to do so, banks may manufacture credit currency to finance these opportunities, and the result may be an inflationary boom with an unfortunate aftermath of financial stringency, crisis, panic, and depression. Nordin and Salera put it this way:

> Hence, we say that the acceleration principle interacts with the multiplier to produce instability in the economy. *Such instability is inherent in the system,* as opposed to being the product of poor business judgment . . . We shall see that the *government, which means all of us in the community,* can do much to smooth out the fluctuations.[5] (Italics supplied.)

In the words of Samuelson, "As far as total investment or money-spending power is concerned, the system is without any thermostat," ". . . it is in the lap of the gods."[6]

The Menace of the "Mature Economy"

In an economy with an open frontier, a high rate of invention, and a growing population, say the

8

Keynesians, the opportunities may be sufficient to cause entrepreneurs to bid for and borrow all of the funds which consumers want to save.

In a more "mature" economy, however, like the United States since 1929, these economists say, investments are not so likely to keep pace with the amount individuals try to save. First, the field for investment shrinks, at least compared to what people try to save. Second, what they try to save (their "propensity to save") increases as average incomes rise and as more of the income goes to the well-to-do, who have a high "propensity to save."

Eventually, therefore, a time comes in "mature" capitalism, when the opportunities for investment fail to keep pace with the amounts individuals put aside as savings. When this happens, uninvested savings pile up in the banks. Some of the currency, then, no longer circulates; and total spending declines. Meanwhile, entrepreneurs have paid out money as income to producers. Now only a part of this money comes back to them in purchase of goods. In other words, entrepreneurs' receipts fall below their expenses. The difference (equal to the uninvested savings) constitutes a business loss. Entrepreneurs must then reduce their future expenditures by that amount. They lay off workers, cut dividends, and otherwise reduce their outlays for production. This reduces the incomes of wage earners, stockholders, and others. Out of these lower incomes, presumably, individuals will not try to save so much as formerly, and the decline in incomes continues until savings are once more brought down into line with investments.

At this new point of equilibrium, however, a large part of the labor force may be unemployed. This unemployment will persist until something happens to increase total spending again. This "something" might be a series of revolutionary inventions to create new opportunities for investment. But this, says Samuelson, leaves the system "in the lap of the gods." How much more sensible it would be for government to come to the rescue with a "compensatory fiscal and monetary policy"!

Government to the rescue!

Says Theodore Morgan in his readable *Income and Employment*, "To set the responsibility for attaining and maintaining full employment on the shoulders of individual consumers or individual businessmen is absurd."[7] According to Samuelson, "The private economy is often like a machine without an effective steering wheel or governor. Compensatory fiscal policy tries to introduce such a governor or thermostatic control device."[8]

This "compensatory fiscal policy" includes two sorts of measures: (1) measures to reduce "the propensity to save," and (2) measures to increase private and government spending.

(1) In order to reduce the propensity to save, Key-

nesians urge that "we" increase "social-consumption expenditures." By this they mean that government should extend the "social security" program. Lawrence Klein, in *The Keynesian Revolution*, writes:

> We need a non-profit institution like the government which can provide a comprehensive, minimum program of social security *in order to reduce the propensity to save.* This program *must cover the entire population,* and it *must cover all those contingencies* which cause people to save on a large scale for the future.[9] (Italics supplied.)

Samuelson, discussing social security payments by government, asks, "Are such expenditures really capitalistic?" Here is his answer:

> We shall later see that "on the first round," these expenditures do not directly consume goods and services; but by swelling the purchasing power of their recipients, they do, "on the second round," create orders and jobs for free private enterprise. However, the thing to note is that the production induced by this process is both privately produced and privately consumed.[10]

According to Samuelson, therefore, we still have capitalism as long as the title to the means of production remains with private persons even though government takes and redistributes the income and fruits of the property on the basis of need or political pressure. This reasoning enables Keynesian economists to profess ardent loyalty to private enterprise and private property while they call for various government measures (e.g., heavily progressive taxes on incomes) for confiscating the fruits of both.

11

(2) In order to raise the rate of private investment and spending, Keynesian economists propose that government aid "small business," subsidize home building, compel licensing of patents, and reduce interest rates.

However, it is by government spending, rather than by private investment, that these economists hope to put back into circulation the "enormously high" savings that Americans try to accumulate. Lorie Tarshis, for example, in his textbook, *The Elements of Economics,* contends that the United States "cannot long maintain full employment through high private investment, because its stock of capital equipment will rise rapidly toward the danger point. . . ." This Stanford University professor goes on to say:

> It seems to be an almost impossible task to raise private investment to the astronomical figure that is now needed; and an even harder problem to keep it there.[11]

Therefore, more and more government spending is necessary to keep private enterprise going.

"Public investment medicine . . . can cure"

"If we take enough of this public investment medicine," Tarshis writes, "it appears that we can cure any depression, so long as we are willing to keep on taking it." And Tarshis explains that by government "investment" he means all government purchases of goods and services, from hiring tax collectors to building monuments.[12]

12

These authors propose that government try to spend for useful objects, like power plants and public housing, roads and schools.

Nevertheless, they agree with Keynes who said, "if the education of our statesmen in the principles of classical economics stands in the way of anything better" even a war or an earthquake may serve to enrich a nation. Samuelson says that there should never be any need for government to spend for boondoggling purposes in view of the many useful projects available. As compared with building pyramids or digging holes and filling them up, "Properly planned useful public works have just as favorable secondary effects, and in addition they fill important human needs." But he stresses the idea that unemployment is a worse evil than government waste. "The one way that the American people should not want to spend their income is upon involuntary [sic] unemployment."[13]

The Keynesian view of investment

Theodore Morgan puts the same idea more plainly:

> ... even from the point of view of output, it is better to employ men in digging holes and filling them up than not to employ them at all; it is better to employ men to make products which we thereupon dump in the middle of the ocean than to leave them idle.

He agrees with Keynes: "Pyramid-building, earthquakes, even wars may serve to increase wealth."[14]

13

Giving money to foreigners, says Tarshis, is a form of "investment," even though we get nothing in return. To make the point so plain that not even the most bored sophomore should miss it, he writes:

> If we could only export one of the printing presses used for the manufacture of Federal Reserve Notes to, let us say, China, our foreign investment would be enormously higher.[15]

This makes even war an "investment" and a means of enrichment, insofar as it gives employment to workers who would "otherwise" be idle.

Among useful government "investments," these economists propose public housing, rural electrification, airfields, more TVAs, Federal aid to education, and government grants or loans to foreign countries. The student will find in Keynesian textbooks little objection to any government "investment" except the possibilty that it may temporarily reduce employment by discouraging timid investors in competing private industries.

Keynesians want fiat money

Government spending stimulates private employment and production, according to "the new economics," even if it is financed by new taxes. But to be fully effective in expanding employment, government should finance its "investments" in some way that does not at the same time take funds from private hands.

14

Therefore, Keynesians prefer that government finance its compensatory spending by manufacturing currency, especially deposit currency (bank credit). "The manufacture of money by banks," says Morgan, "is a cheap and simple process," and this is the process these authors recommend.[16]

However, if banks are to lend funds and create deposits whenever government gives the word, they must forget about their gold reserves and their responsibility for paying out gold on demand. In other words, the Keynesian proposal for "compensatory"' deficit spending by government implies abandonment of the gold standard in favor of a "managed currency," that is, inconvertible paper money, or fiat currency.

Keynesian economists know this to be true. Therefore, they belittle and berate the gold standard in terms that remind one of William Jennings Bryan and his "cross of gold." Samuelson says that the gold standard "made each country a slave rather than the master of its own economic destiny."[17] Tarshis ridicules it by comparing it unfavorably with a limburger cheese standard.[18]

And more controls to check inflation

These economists admit that their "loan-expenditure" policy may cause rising prices and currency depreciation under a fiat ("managed") currency. Some of them say that a little inflation is a good thing, but all of them agree that a people may easily get too much of it. To prevent this, they propose increased government authority over credit, interest rates, wages, and prices. As Klein says, "There is no reason why intelligent economic planning cannot be of just the correct amount, that amount which gives permanent full employment and stable prices."

> There are several administrative methods of gaining full employment without inducing inflation. If the economic planners are given *complete control* over the government fiscal policy so that they can *spend when and where spending is needed* to stimulate employment and *tax when and where taxation is needed* to halt upward price movements, there will be no problem of associated inflationary dangers.[19] (Italics supplied.)

This means that "the planners" would control every individual's income and expenditures.

The alternative to such planning, says Klein, is government wage and price control. He appears not to realize that abolishing the free market restricts individual liberty fully as much as the "complete control" over fiscal policy, which he admits is inconsistent with present political institutions in the United States. Instead, he writes that:

> The OPA served us beyond all best hopes and wishes during the war, and it did not infringe upon any fundamental liberties, only upon the liberty of greedy profiteering. This organization can serve us also in peace.[20]

In order to avoid the two extremes of mass unemployment or destructive inflation, therefore, Klein

16

offers us either an authority with "complete control" over government spending and taxes, or general price control.

Samuelson says that "when everything is 'short' relative to demand and full-employment capacity, reliance on the price mechanism is inequitable and gives rise to an endless inflationary spiral with grave economic consequences." At such times, he says, the price mechanism must be "supplemented" by direct controls and rationing.[21]

Keynes proposed to prevent inflation by forced savings, in addition to tax increases, subsidies, price control and rationing.

Following the master, then, these economists urge that government manage the currency and credit, control saving and investment, fix prices and incomes, ration commodities, constantly expand government industries and "investments," and provide for every individual in sickness, accident, unemployment, immaturity, old age, and death. And this is to be the program in time of peace as in time of war.

"We owe it to ourselves"

One of the chief road-blocks which Keynesians see in the loan-expenditure route to prosperity is the businessman's fear of mounting government debt. This fear, they assure us, is not well founded. Rapidly increasing debt is merely a price we pay for prosperity, says Tarshis.

17

If we do not want high debt, high interest rates, high wages, and high prices, then in effect we do not want high employment and prosperity.[22]

"The only question, then," Tarshis continues, "is whether the government can always find a lender or someone who will accept government bonds."

In the final analysis this is no problem for the simple reason that the government controls the Federal Reserve Banks and can always compel them to buy government bonds. Anyone who controls a bank and is free to make the rules under which it operates will have no trouble in borrowing money. The government is in precisely this position, and therefore can always secure funds.

There is no sign that a high debt exhausts the credit of the government of the United States. And since as a last resource "it can borrow from itself," there need be no fear on this account.[23]

Klein agrees: "An internally held public debt can never be a burden, because we owe it to ourselves."[24]

On this point, however, Samuelson dissents. He notes that a large public debt may be a burden even though "we owe it to ourselves." Even if the people that paid the taxes were the same ones who received the interest payments on the government bonds, yet the taxes might reduce incentive to work and produce. But he goes on to say:

In dispassionately analyzing the growth of the debt, one error we must avoid: we must not forget that the real national product of the United States is an ever-growing thing.

For this reason, he says, "the public debt might in-

18

crease by 250 billion dollars in 25 years without its relative percentage burden growing." This would, he claims, permit an average deficit of 10 billion dollars per year before it would be necessary to turn to printing money or selling interest-free bonds to the Federal Reserve Banks.[25]

The debt burden and inflation

A skeptic might ask whether the real national product will continue to increase, as Samuelson so confidently expects it will, under the policies of the "mixed economy" which he and other Keynesians endorse and advocate. He might also ask why Samueleson believes a 10-billion dollar deficit in future will not lead to printing money or selling interest-free bonds to the Federal Reserve Banks, whereas much smaller deficits in the past led to large issues of paper money in this country and necessitated large purchases of government securities at nominal interest rates.

Theodore Morgan, like Samuelson, admits that a government debt might be burdensome, even though "we owe it to ourselves," but he suggests that the government ease the burden by permitting a little price inflation. He suggests that a rise of 1 or 2 per cent per year in the general price level would be beneficially stimulating to the economy, and at the same time it would ease the burden of the debt on taxpayers.[26]

This proposed rise in prices would correspondingly reduce the buying power for owners of many kinds of property and for persons with fixed incomes. In effect, therefore, Morgan proposes a discriminatory capital levy of 1 or 2 per cent every year on the owners of bank deposits, bonds, and other fixed-income properties, together with a special income tax increasing each year by the same per cent on persons living on pensions, insurance benefits, and salaries.

Any "easing" of the debt burden and any "stimulus" to the economy would result from this expropriation of salaried persons, pensioners, bond holders, and beneficiaries of life insurance policies and endowments.

This indifference to property rights shown by Theodore Morgan is typical of Keynesian economists.

II. Keynesism and Socialism

What is this thing called "freedom"?

Since Keynesians advocate so many forms of government intervention in the name of "full employment," it is not surprising to find them favoring it for other purposes. If government should take a man's earnings because he wants to save too much, why should it not take them on the ground merely that someone else needs or wants them? If government should build power plants to give employment, why not also railways and steel mills? Economists of the new order can only echo, "Why not?"

Theodore Morgan says that "Probably, majority opinion agrees with our own national policy that the right of a man to engage in business for himself is not a basic freedom." All modern economies, he continues, are mixtures of government and private enterprise, and the proper dividing line between the two can be fixed only by time and experience, which "will serve to correct our social judgments."[27] This is typical of the attitude of Keynesian economists, as well as of many scholars who are neither Keynesians nor economists.

Is this attitude consistent with constitutional safeguards for individual rights, or liberty? Time is "the stuff life is made of," said Poor Richard. The time government takes in an experiment with the properties and jobs of individuals can never be put back into the lives of those whom its policies affect. Repeal of an unjust law can never undo the injustices inflicted by it. Dislodging the vested interests in a government activity is even more difficult than dispossessing private owners.

Socialism not a menace to freedom?

According to Samuelson, a "survey of history shows" that the degree of political freedom and civil liberty which citizens may possess has little or nothing to do with the extent of government control over the economy. For example, he says, "Britain, Scandinavia, and other socialist countries have retained all of the familiar civil liberties and individual political freedoms that are guaranteed by our own Constitution."[28] But are not property rights among the most important of all civil liberties which constitutions and representative institutions are designed to protect? Is not protection of property rights necessary in order to give value and meaning to "political freedom"?

Instead of dealing with such questions as these in his discussion of the "Isms" (fascism, communism, and socialism), Samuelson plunges on into a long section entitled, "The use of an over-all pricing system under socialism and capitalism." In it, the author analyzes "the problem of pricing in a planned socialist state."

From such a study of socialism, he says, "we are in a position to see what friendly and unfriendly critics think is wrong in our present system . . ." and "We gain an introduction to problems of 'welfare economics,' i.e., to the study of what is considered right and wrong concerning any economic system." Thus, he continues, "the economist, as disinterested observer, may help to throw light upon how successfully an economic system realizes any suggested ethical *goals*."[29]

As it turns out, the only "ethical goals" he considers are those of the Socialist: equality of income and "social dividends" to the needy.

What is missing from this picture?

When an author uses socialism as his standard for judging capitalism, and when he concludes that capitalism is the system to be reformed, does he not run the risk that readers may think he regards socialism as the ideal system?

The one system which Samuelson flatly rejects and condemns is laissez faire, to which he attributes various widespread evils: "wasteful exhaustion of irreplaceable natural resources," "periodic business crises," "extremes of poverty and wealth," "corruption of government by vested interest groups," and

23

"too often . . . all-consuming [sic] monopoly."[30]

Yet, when the same author discusses government regulation and ownership in the American "mixed" economy or elsewhere, he finds only abuses of what liberty may remain and little or nothing of abuses or evils of government intervention.

Nothing, for example, of government waste of resources, human and material.

Nothing of political corruption among those with a vested interest in government spending and government subsidies.

Nothing of the restrictions and inefficiency of government monopolies, government price controls, and government allocations.

Nothing of the huge losses already inflicted upon savers and investors by interventionist policies, only a mild warning of possible, future dangers.

Nothing of the frauds and character destruction among recipients of social security.

Nothing of the decline in levels of living and work under socialism in Britain, or the growing shortage and high cost of venture capital in the American "mixed" economy.

Nothing of the fact that fascism was a development of the Keynesian managed-economy, full-employment idea, an attempt to subject the individual to the "collective conscience" which Samuelson sets up as arbiter for our own government's policy.

In order to judge the impartiality of a book or its probable effect on the mind of a student, one must

24

know what the author leaves out as well as what he includes. In Samuelson's text, the best-seller among all elementary textbooks in economics, one finds little or no mention of the many uneconomic results which competent economists attribute to government intervention in the American "mixed" economy. Instead, he says:

> I should like to conclude on a note of profound optimism. The American economy is in better shape in the 1950's than it ever was in the past. . . . Our mixed economy — wars aside — has a great future before it.[31]

Collectivism vs. individualism

Not only do the authors of the "new economics" largely ignore the evils which some of us believe flow from government intervention; not only do they attribute the imperfections of the mixed economy to capitalism rather than to governmentalism; but one looks in vain for any principle by which to distinguish between individual right and government authority.

The only guide that they recognize is not a principle but "social preferences," "society's appraisal," "correct social planning," "democratic decisions,' or a "collective conscience."[32]

Nordin and Salera typify this Keynesian tendency to ignore notions of individual right when they casually remark that government "means all of us in the community."[33] Thus these writers set up "Society"— the collective—as an entity in which the individual submerges and dissolves. In this view, justice means whatever "the collective conscience" dictates.

Is it fair to call this a *collectivistic* point of view? Let us contrast it with the individualist view. The individualist considers "society" to mean those relations which individuals enter into with one another as they seek to satisfy their individual wants. Justice means protection of each individual's liberty, or right, to work out his destiny free from interference or expropriation by others. The function of government is to adminster justice, that is, to preserve freedom, not to dictate activities. And government means, not "society" or "all of us," but those persons designated to prevent each individual from interfering with the liberty of any other.

What everyone owns, no one owns

To the individualist, therefore, there is a serious fallacy in Professor Samuelson's statement that "socialism, almost by definition, means a society in which most land and capital goods or nonhuman resources of all kinds are *owned collectively by society. . . .*"[34] (Italics supplied.) Society in the sense of relations between individuals is not people but certain ways persons act, or certain aspects of their actions. In this sense, society cannot own anything because it is an abstraction, not persons. Neither can society in the sense of "all the people" own anything. What everyone possesses, like a view of the sun, no one owns, for no one can appropriate it for his own use to the exclusion of others, and such appropriation for exclusive use is the essence of property rights, or ownership.

What socialism means

What socialism really means is that government officials administer wealth taken from, or donated by, private owners. These officials may set up in business with this wealth and trade it (or the services of it) for other goods produced by private enterprise. Even to call this government administration of wealth "government ownership" is a loose use of terms, but not so misleading as to call it "social ownership," or "collective ownership."

Similarly revealing is the passage in Samuelson's book in which he presents as a paradox the fact that fascist regimes "have often passed socialistic measures." This is not a paradox at all, for fascism was (or is) a form of socialism similar to British socialism or to the managed-currency, welfare state proposed by American Keynesians.

Frequently, especially in his 1951 edition, Samuelson puts his criticisms of capitalism in the third person: "Social reformers attach great importance to . . ." "society now rules that . . ." "friendly and unfriendly critics think . . ." "democratic countries are not satisfied with . . ." "the collective conscience of the American people" and so on.

Whether or not these imaginary authorities express the author's own opinions, the reader may judge for himself. In reaching that judgment, he must consider whether the author chooses his spokesmen mainly from one side of the argument, and whether, when he fails to quote an opposing view, he himself gives an effective answer to the "critics" or "social reformers" he professes to quote.

At one point, however, one may be excused, perhaps, for suspecting that his disguise slipped a little. That is where he refers to his socialist spokesmen as "perfectionists."[35]

Again, I should like to ask, is it not fair to call this "social" point of view a "collectivist" one? Or even "socialist"?

Of course, this label does not necessarily mean that the point of view is unsound; but classification of anything is a step toward appraisal.

The "New Economics" and Marxian Socialism

From the foregoing, one may see that Keynesism has several points in common with Marxian Socialism. Among these are:

1 the theory that the rate of return on investments tends to decline and unemployment tends to increase in a free-enterprise, capitalistic economy;

2 emphasis on the depressing influence of savings in a "mature" capitalistic economy;

3 theories of an irresistible tendency to monopoly, increasing concentration of wealth, and the doom of free markets in free enterprise, or laissez faire;

4 disparagement of individual enterprise and responsibility in favor of government control over savings and provision for old age, unemployment, and other emergencies in an elaborate "social security" program;

5 proposals for "progressive" income and inheritance taxes;

6 proposals for government management of the currency and banking, for government ownership of certain industries; and for liquidation ("euthanasia") of the *rentier* (bond-holding and fixed-income) classes;

7 a collectivistic view of property rights as privileges from the State, to be given or taken away at the will of the State;

8 a tendency to identify government with "all of us," or with "society," in the democratic socialist state and in the democratic Keynesian "mixed" economy;

9 a tendency to deal with persons and economic activity in terms of "classes," "averages," "aggregates," and technological or economic "forces";

10 a mechanistic view of human behavior as predictable and controllable by government, through

study and manipulation of interest rates, money, government lending and spending, taxation, and technological developments.

The Keynesian theories are skilfully presented

Yet, despite the similarities between Marxian socialism and Keynesism and despite growing hostility to Russian Marxists, the Keynesian national-income approach makes rapid headway in American colleges and universities. Why? Is it because of the attractive wrappings in which economists of the Keynesian persuasion present their package of ideas?

First, they claim, no doubt sincerely, that they come, not to destroy capitalism, but to save it. Consequently, they get a hearing in places which would be closed to professed Socialists.

Second, they support their theory with charts and diagrams that make it look scientific and exact. They use technical terms and mathematical formulas, as a professional magician uses his stage props, to produce conclusions that disbelieving laymen are unable to refute. They make liberal use of government statistics on national income, savings, investment, consumer spending, and the like. Many people regard these figures as precise and highly significant, so that the proposal to use them as guides for "compensatory fiscal and monetary policy" appears simple and practicable.

Third, by representing government spending and

deficits as keys to prosperity, "the new economics" gives aid and comfort to everyone who wants government to do something *for* him or *to* his neighbor. For example, Samuelson writes that "to the extent that taxes come out of the income of the more well-to-do and thrifty and are used to make payments to the needy and ready-to-spend — to that extent the total purchasing power is increased."

Furthermore, the appeal of certain Keynesian authors is greater because they write with the dash and vigor that come from a feeling of mission. True, in order to appear merely as disinterested observers, they often use devices such as Samuelson's third-party spokesmen (e.g., "most people will feel that this is only as it should be"[36]). This makes a textbook appeal to teachers who favor the Keynesian point of view but prefer to appear disinterested.

By appropriate labelling or emphasis, a teacher or writer may sway students and readers without seeming to commit himself to any definite position. For example, one may more readily get approval for subsidies by calling them "social dividends," as Samuelson does, than by calling them "doles" as an opponent might do. He may attribute a government policy to "society" or to "the collective conscience of the people" rather than to "government" or to certain "politicians and officials."

Moreover, as I pointed out above, an author creates an effect by what he leaves out as well as by what he puts in. He may himself believe that he is presenting "both sides" fairly, while he leaves out of consideration or pays little attention to the most telling arguments of one side or the other. Or he may treat objections to his views as "problems" to be solved, rather than as possible invalidations. Professor Richard Ruggles, in *An Introduction to National and Income Analysis,* uses this method in dealing with difficulties that might be met in applying the Keynesian theory.

Yet, although these writers may adopt a pose of non-partisanship on details of theory or practice, they boldly urge the main outlines of a program that must have far-reaching results in every phase of human affairs. Toward the beginning of his text, Samuelson flatly asserts that:

> . . . it is part of the government's function to alleviate one of the most important causes of acute and chronic cycles in unemployment or inflation. Especially in communities like our own, individuals as a whole may try to save much more or much less than the private enterprise can profitably or usefully invest in new real capital goods. . . . Clearly the government must try to use its constitutional fiscal and monetary powers to enable private enterprise to maintain a steady level of high employment. . . .[37]

Thus in a few words he sets forth a government policy that must reach into the minutest details of the life and work of every citizen.

For government can control *total* savings, investment, and income only by interfering with myriads of *individual* acts which make up the totals. An over-all restriction of bank credit, for example, or a tax increase, directly *coerces* individual citizens into changing their plans and conduct in countless ways.

In general, moveover, Keynesian proposals for "compensatory" policies follow Marxian Socialism in seeking to *force* individuals to obey the rule, "From everyone according to his abilities, to everyone according to his needs." Arguments and theories used to support these proposals are essentially Marxian.

Yet, we cannot show the fallacy of Keynesism merely by noting its far-reaching implications or its resemblance to Marxian socialism. Therefore, let us look at two recent works representative of two points of view common among free-enterprise critics of the doctrine.

The first, *The Economics of Illusion,* by Dr. L. A. Hahn, presents the "neo-classical" view that rejects the Keynesian over-saving theory of business depressions and urges return to free markets, but accepts government control of currency and credit as a means of stabilizing business or reviving it after a crisis and depression.

The second, *Economics and the Public Welfare,* by Dr. B. M. Anderson, with a wealth of supporting data, sets forth the classical, laissez faire view that government intervention is the chief enemy of economic stability, progress, and prosperity.

III. Recent Criticisms of "The New Economics"

IN ITS ESSENTIALS the so-called "new economics" is almost as old as the use of money. Again and again it has been used to justify government extravagance and to defend schemes for debasing the coinage or inflating the currency. It was the theory John Law persuaded the government of France to let him try out in the early 18th Century. The result was the Mississippi Bubble, the best-known boom and bust of recorded history up to 1929. In the 19th Century, Lauderdale, Malthus, Sismondi, and J. A. Hobson advanced much the same views, not to mention Karl Marx and his disciples. Keynes did little if anything more than use new terms for old ideas.

"Keynesianism is a sin of my youth"

A well-known, present-day economist, however, Dr. L. A. Hahn, claims the doubtful honor of having refurbished and reissued what he now regards as this fool's gold of economic theories. In a book of essays entitled *The Economics of Illusion*, Dr. Hahn confesses that "Keynesianism is a sin of my youth," which he committed several years before Keynes got credit for it.[38]

As a young economist and banker in Germany in 1920, Hahn ardently espoused the idea that easy credit policies are necessary to keep a modern economy fully stimulated and working at top speed. Without this stimulus, he believed, it would get clogged with unused purchasing power, or savings. The result would be unemployment and idle factories. A few years later, as he saw the results of these easy-money policies, he came to regard inflation as a worse evil than deflation. Therefore, he re-examined his theories and concluded he had been mostly wrong in his original explanation for depressions.

The causes of business depression he now finds, not in oversaving, but in a necessary readjustment after a preceding credit inflation. In addition, he says, depressions may be aggravated and prolonged by policies which prevent reduction of costs after the excesses of the boom are liquidated. These policies are mainly: (1) wage rigidities protected by unions and wage-hour laws; (2) burdensome taxes on enterprise; and (3) government restrictions on trade and production, such as tariffs, crop controls, exchange restrictions, and price controls.

Keynesism as "The Economics of Illusion"

At first, says Hahn, currency-and-credit inflation speeds up spending and increases employment. This is because certain costs (e.g., wage rates, rents, and interest charges) lag behind selling prices of the products. This stimulating effect, however, lasts only until the lagging costs catch up to the rise in prices— as they soon do. After that, further inflation only raises the general price level and reduces confidence in the currency. Eventually it must result in a flight of capital, which in turn sets off a degenerative spiral of growing unemployment, currency inflation, rising prices, and further export of capital.

Therefore, Hahn says, the Keynesian theory that currency inflation and increased spending can increase employment is valid only if one assumes a lag in wages, and this lag will continue only as long as wage earners can be kept in ignorance of what is going on.

> For it [the Keynesian view] presupposes an economy whose members do not see through the changes brought about by monetary or fiscal manipulation — or as some might say, the swindle. Above all, it presupposes that people are blinded by the idea that the value of money is stable — by the "money illusion." . . .[39]

Hence he calls Keynesism, "the economics of illusion."

Inflation encourages uneconomic policy

Most people will agree with Hahn that a policy which depends on such an illusion has little chance of success today in a nation of free discussion and collective bargaining. In fact, union wage demands now generally run ahead of any increase in over-all spending, at least in the United States.

Some Keynesians recognize this, at least as a possibility. Samuelson, for example, says that the possibility that wages and prices may begin to soar as spending increases, even though there is still unemployment and excess capacity, is "America's greatest problem and challenge." "If businessmen and trade-unions react perversely to an increased demand, fiscal policy cannot be relied upon to achieve and maintain full employment."[40] The alternatives he offers, if "business, labor and agriculture" do not learn to curb their demands, are: (1) a reserve army of 10 million jobless; (2) continued inflation; or (3) government price and wage controls which "would involve a degree of planning incompatible with past, and probably present, philosophical beliefs of the great majority of the American people."

Yet, one looks in vain in this leading textbook for suggestions that "business, labor and agriculture" may restore free markets, at least in domestic trade, or that it would help if they did. "Laissez faire is dead! Long live compensatory and fiscal policy!"

It is here that Hahn takes issue with the Keynesian view. He argues that: (1) there cannot be chronic underinvestment in free markets; and (2) the remedy for chronic unemployment is the return to a free labor market and removal of trade barriers.

When government uses an easy-money policy to cure unemployment caused by too-high wage rates or monopolistic price-maintenance, he says, it encourages the unioneers and monopolists to continue their uneconomic policies. Thus it perpetuates and aggravates the very evils that are the root of the trouble. Eventually, these forces get out of control and the result is the catastrophe of a runaway inflation.

Hahn concedes the case for a "managed currency"

In *The Economics of Illusion,* Hahn pursues the Keynesians in the twists and turns of their dialectics to ferret out some of their inconsistencies and fallacies. At times his pursuit is successful, and he is one of the best-known critics of Keynesian doctrines, a sincere advocate of private enterprise.

In the course of his argument, however, like many other critics of government intervention, Dr. Hahn gives away his own cause against "compensatory fiscal and monetary policy." He recommends that government use deficit spending to stimulate business in the recovery phase of the business cycle, and he condemns the "hyper-classicism of those who opposed attempts at reflation" in the early 1930s.

What Hahn objects to, therefore, is not a compensatory fiscal and monetary policy, but bad timing in applying it and neglect of other devices, such as abolishing restrictions on free markets. He writes:

In order to restore confidence in the price structure,

the government is justified in compensating, and even obliged to compensate, the lacking private demand by proper expenditures for which it acquires the means by loans not by taxes.[42]

But who is to decide when the producers have completed the necessary adjustments and thus merited a helping hand from government? If government recognizes that the time for recovery has arrived, why don't investors? Does government get a sudden access of wisdom in the trough of a depression?

And how is the government to borrow the money for its compensatory spending?

Here Hahn accepts the Keynesian view that the gold standard must be repudiated. He agrees with the Keynesians that the central-bank authorities should fix discount rates and determine lending policies according to their estimates of domestic credit needs rather than according to the need for protecting gold reserves against a possible "flight of capital" to foreign countries.

In place of the gold standard, Hahn favors a "money-free" economy, in which bank deposits are as good as cash (legal tender), and there is always plenty of legal-tender money to take care of all possible bank runs. Then individuals' desire for liquidity, he says, cannot cause deflation because the government can supply the banks with enough paper money so that they need never refuse loans or liquidate investments in order to get cash to pay off their depositors. This, he says, will make Keynes's "liquidity-preference" concept an anachronism.[43]

One might add that it would also open the door for what Hahn himself considers unsound credit policy. For example, it was this self-same "money-free" policy which caused the inflationary boom of the 1920s. Under government urging and government orders, the central banks of almost all countries fostered an era of easy money (credit) in order to finance public works and deficits in government industries, to prop up various forms of economic disequilibrium which arose out of World War I, to maintain prices and wage rates for over-expanded industries, and to maintain confidence despite the unbalance and the unsound use of credit.

This story—the record of government's role in the boom-and-bust of 1920-1932 has so far been told best by the late Benjamin M. Anderson, in his *Economics and the Public Welfare,* published just after his death in 1949. In this eye-witness account of the period, 1913-1946, Dr. Anderson shows the futility of Hahn's hope that government control of currency and credit can lead to a "sound" credit policy or increased financial stability.

"When government plays God"

Dr. Anderson originally titled his book "When Government Plays God." His friends vetoed this title on the ground that it might hurt the sales of the book in academic circles where it is usually necessary to appear disinterested. Doubtless his friends were right, but Dr. Anderson, I think, believed that it was not a virtue to be disinterested about the results of government currency management, which apostles of "the new economics" advocate.

At any rate, "When Government Plays God" describes the theme of the book.[44] Seldom have facts been so marshalled to show the progress of a plausible fallacy in wreaking havoc with the economic life, not merely of one nation, but of every nation. That fallacy is the easy-money, deficit-spending theory of the New Deal and of the Keynesian economists: the theory that government may promote prosperity by taking steps to increase the quantity of currency, bank credit, and unproductive spending.

The New Deal before Franklin Roosevelt

Dr. Anderson dates the first phase of the New Deal in the United States from 1924, the year in which a Federal Administration of this country dictated an easy-money policy ("an immense artificial manipulation of the money market"). According to the author's own account, however, he might have dated it from 1917, for as he shows, the United States Government used this banking system, its own creature, to help finance the inflation of World War I and the postwar boom of 1919-20.[45] True, the Federal Reserve Banks regained some independence of action in 1920, but their tardy and moderate increases in rediscount rates in that year were blamed for the depression which followed, and thereafter they were never again free from political direction and interference.

Dr. Anderson tells vividly and in detail how this political domination of bank policies brought about the runaway stock market boom of the late 1920s. Then he goes on to show how the subsequent crash and depression were intensified and prolonged by "frantic governmental economic planning" which began even while the stock market crash was going on. For the most part his account is as clear and readable as a newspaper account of a bank holdup.

"It was dishonor"

And a bank holdup is what the United States Government staged in 1933 when it seized depositors' gold and gave the President authority to issue inconvertible paper money and reduce the gold value of the dollar. After quoting Senator Carter Glass concerning the immorality and fraud of these acts, Dr. Anderson says:

> To the grand old Senator, morality was something written in the Heavens, eternal and unchangeable. But the pragmatic philosopher . . . was no less shocked than the Senator. There is no need in human life so great as that men should trust one another and should trust their government, should believe in promises, and should keep promises that future promises may be believed in and in order that confident cooperation may be possible. Good

faith — personal, national, and international — is the first prerequisite of decent living, of the steady going on of industry, of government financial strength, and of international peace.

The President's course in connection with the gold standard and in connection with the Thomas Amendment, represented an act of absolute bad faith. . . . The Government was bound by its solemn promises, and the President was personally bound by his campaign utterances and by the platform of his party. It was dishonor.[46]

Thus the moral indignation of an economist who saw that trust and good faith are the foundations of all human cooperation broke forth in bitter condemnation of those who sought to promote prosperity by deceit and spoliation.

Yet indignation must be governed by understanding. It is Anderson's detailed and expert examination of the financial record that gives his *Economics and the Public Welfare* its authoritative weight and penetration as a critique of Keynesian proposals for an inconvertible currency and deficit spending.

Government control must be "political"

In this clear and detailed moving picture, however, one may find something of which even its producer was scarcely aware. As Anderson describes the inflation of 1924-29, he attributes it solely to the "weakness and bad judgment" of certain Federal officials in yielding to political influences. He suggests that "stronger" men would have done better.

But was it mere accident that the control over the Federal Reserve System was in the hands of "weak" men? Will any administration long tolerate government officials (e.g., members of the Federal Reserve Board) who show good financial judgment instead of good political judgment?

Many persons, like Senator Glass and Dr. Anderson, who strongly favor private enterprise in banking as a general rule, make an exception in favor of government "control" of central bank policy. They see the many advantages of close cooperation among individual banks. One obvious way of getting this cooperation is for government to set up a banker's bank, like the Bank of England or the Bank of France (both of which used to be privately owned). But, when government sets up such a bank and gives it a monopoly of certain functions, it creates a special privilege and a corresponding political obligation. Therefore, most advocates of a central-bank monopoly propose that this bank must be "regulated" by government as a public utility.

The founders of the Federal Reserve System in 1913 were warned of the danger of political control of such banks, but they hoped to prevent political "abuses" by such devices as that of permitting the private bank members to elect most of the directors of the 12 Federal Reserve Banks, and by giving long-term appointments to the members of the Federal Reserve Board. Most classical economists, even among those most devoted to free enterprise, still cling to the belief that somehow the monetary system can be managed by such a government-appointed board which, "like the Supreme Court," is free from political influence.

Careful reading of Dr. Anderson's book should shake that belief, especially if one keeps in mind also the outcome of the Reconstruction Finance Corporation to which Anderson seems to have given approval. As *Economics and the Public Welfare* makes clear, the Federal Reserve officials have usually been among the ablest and most honest persons that could be found. They did not act politically because they were weak; they were not disloyal to their trust. Instead, they were faithful to the *political* trust of those who appointed them.

This is not to say that all central banking must be political in nature or policy. But such central banks as *government* sets up and controls must serve political purposes. Failure to recognize this fact, or to make it clear, is the one serious flaw in Anderson's otherwise penetrating analysis.

Excessive bank credit in the 1920s

What Anderson did see and make clear, as few economists do, is the fallacy of the Keynesian "purchasing power theory." This is the theory that lack of spending is the cause of large-scale unemployment and depression, and that government should intervene to assure enough money and spending to maintain at all times the demand for labor and goods.

Anderson counters this theory with the fact that bank credit was more than sufficient in the 1920s due to the very sort of government intervention that the Keynesians recommend. This over-abundance of bank credit caused investment to run ahead of savings, and gave rise to a disastrous boom and bust.

Next he goes on to show how the processes of production and trade themselves generate a sufficient quantity of credit whenever free markets are given a chance to develop the *equilibrium* necessary for a good *quality* of credit.

Credit in free markets: an incomplete exchange

In free markets, credit arises when one person transfers to another his services and goods, or valid claims on services and goods, in return for a promise to pay later. A seller advances credit when he lets a buyer take and use goods before paying for them. A wage earner gives credit to his employer when he works for a week or two before pay day.

Credit is not, therefore, a matter of bank checks, banknotes, or figures on a bank's books. These are merely records of credit transactions, not credit itself. Credit is an incomplete exchange of goods.

When government does not control banking, except to enforce contracts, *well-managed* banks serve only as credit *brokers*, not as credit *manufacturers*. They record credit transactions and act as clearing houses and agents for credit developed and used by individuals and business firms. They keep books for the real manufacturers of credit, who are the producers and exchangers of goods and services.

Credit develops with trade

Producers and dealers may create and use credit with little or no resort to banks. In certain sections of the United States in the first half of the 19th Century, banks were often hard to reach. Some states actually prohibited private banks by law. In those places, business developed with comparatively little bank credit, and even with comparatively little money. Merchants bought the products of farmers and artisans, giving in return purchase-orders good at their shops. In that case, the producers sold the goods on credit to the merchant. The credit was liquidated when these producers used their purchase-orders to buy other goods from the merchant. If the merchant owned a stock of goods to begin with, he could sell on credit to producers, and they could discharge their debts later by selling their goods to him in return for their own I.O.U.s.

In such a society, the volume of credit obviously depended on the amount of goods produced and exchanged. This amount, in turn, depended on the efficiency of producers and merchants—their ambition, inventiveness, ability to cooperate, richness of soil—and on one other thing: *trust*.

Banks register credits

Trust came as a sequel to competence and honesty. Competence and honesty developed as suppression of violence and enforcement of contracts created a favorable political environment for production and trade.

When these conditions are present—honor, trust, and a fund or flow of goods — there is credit. The supply of credit rises and falls with the amount of exchangeable goods produced, and this amount depends on the efficiency of producers and dealers. It does not matter whether the goods are commodities or services, durable or perishable, consumers' goods or producers' goods (tools and machinery), the *quantity* of credit in free markets depends on its *quality* as measured by its command over goods. This quality in turn, depends on the faithfulness with which producers and traders meet one another's expectations in production, trade, and finance.

Producers do not need the banker, therefore, to *create* credit. He is useful in keeping records and as an agent for producers and traders in ascertaining the credit-worthiness of individuals in particular transactions—when the owners of goods and credit want such service. As his customers gain confidence in his work, they let the banker record more of their credit transactions and let him act as their agent in lending funds that would otherwise be idle. Then the idea may arise that the bank creates the credit.

48

What "inflation" means

If producers sell goods on credit to persons who do not keep their promises to pay for them (perhaps because their plans go awry), there is trouble. The goods are gone and trust is destroyed. Then credit shrinks and people complain of a shortage of credit. At this point, if government has suppressed the gold standard, it may issue more paper money or set up means for using government bonds as a basis for deposit currency. Then it may give or lend this money or currency to otherwise insolvent debtors. In other words, it may monetize debt. This permits creditors and debtors to continue making the bad loans and unproductive investments which caused the losses.

This is the essential meaning and evil of "inflation." It is an expansion of currency for unproductive spending and "investment." One result of it is a decline in the purchasing power of money, that is, a rise in prices. Another result is that those who receive the government's handouts get goods without giving goods or services in exchange. This is what a counterfeiter does.

Of course, individuals are bound to make mistakes in use of credit. They may produce the wrong goods or give credit to dishonest or incompetent persons. In free markets, however, such mistakes carry their own penalty and remedy. Imprudent lenders lose their power to lend, and spendthrift debtors lose their power to borrow. Credit management, therefore, gravitates into the hands of those who learn to use it productively.

The gold standard prevented inflation

Yet, although credit in free markets arises mainly out of production, producers do not ordinarily measure it in terms of bushels of wheat or tons of coal. They state it in terms of the monetary unit in which they price their goods—so many dollars, francs, or pesos. In modern times, when free to choose, they make silver or gold their standard. They state their prices in terms of such standard money, and they prefer to be paid in it or in claims that are readily exchangeable for it. In international trade, gold is the standard, even when governments forbid it in domestic trade, at least between sovereign nations. (The United States has largely destroyed the monetary usefulness of silver by its manipulations of the silver market on behalf of the silver producers.)

Under the gold standard, the banker has another function in addition to that of recording credit transactions and serving as agent in clearing, transferring, and advancing credits. He acts also as a merchant in gold, or a keeper of a warehouse for gold.

Soon after governments (e.g., those of the United States and England in the 19th Century) began to enforce the contracts which bankers and producers made in terms of standard money, the bankers'

50

purchase orders (banknotes and checks) replaced almost all others. "Trading stamps," streetcar tokens, "coupons good only at our store," and occasional "due bills" payable in service or merchandise were instances of purchase orders not convertible into gold at a fixed ratio; but people used these forms of purchase orders for only a small part of the total trade in most countries prior to 1933. When producers were free to choose their own currency, they used mainly one that was readily convertible into standard money at stable, predetermined rates.

When goods were as good as gold

As the gold standard developed, gold became the measure for credit and a means for controlling credit expansion. This was because buyers of goods used it to measure the value of the goods which gave rise to credit. Every producer had to price his goods low enough in terms of the standard money so that buyers would take these goods in preference to the standard commodity, gold. As long as producers used their credit to produce goods that were more desirable than gold, at the prices asked for them, their credit was "good." It was as good as gold.

Under these conditions, banks and other lenders could safely expand credit only as the supplies of gold increased, *or as producers found ways of producing goods that, at the prices asked, buyers preferred to gold.* When they expanded credit faster

51

than this, both borrowers and lenders suffered losses. This means that inflation of currency or credit could not proceed far, under the gold standard, before automatic checks came into play.

Under the gold standard, even government borrowing was deflationary, not inflationary. There were two reasons for this. *First,* it reduced the supply of loan funds available for private borrowers and brought about a rise in rates of interest. *Second,* it caused growing distrust of all credit. This was because government pays its debts out of taxes, which reduce the ability of taxpayers to pay their private debts. Creditors knew this. Therefore, as government debts mounted, they grew more cautious. Eventually they began to convert their bank credits into gold, which they hoarded or shipped out of the country for safe keeping.

This potential demand for gold acted as a brake on the expansion of credit, both government credit and private credit.

It is because of this check-rein effect on currency and prices that Keynesian economists want governments to "abandon" the gold standard. This means that they urge that government prohibit citizens from using gold as money, prohibit the issue of banknotes convertible into gold for domestic use, and prohibit (or refuse to enforce) contracts in terms of gold. In other words, their proposal to "abandon" the gold standard is actually a proposal to *suppress* it.

Gold prevented inflation, not expansion, of credit

Advocates of a "managed currency" contend that gold prevents or impedes expansion of credit. The output of gold, they say may not keep pace with the output of other commodities. If the currency is tied to gold, a lag in gold production must cause a shortage of money and declining prices for other goods. This decline in the general level of prices, they argue, tends to depress industry and employment. Consequently, a shortage of gold is likely to retard economic progress, if a nation remains on the gold standard and tries to maintain a fixed monetary value for gold. It is because of this depressing influence of the gold standard in the past, they claim, that governments so often abandoned it or revalued ("debased") their currencies.

This line of argument, however, ignores several facts:

1 Gold is one of the most widely distributed of all natural resources. It is found in all parts of the globe; and, throughout the centuries, man seems to have found ways of increasing the output of gold about as fast as the output of other goods. There is no evidence that this correlation between the production of gold and the production of other things may not continue indefinitely.

2 Inventions to economize gold usually keep pace with other forms of invention. In freedom, improvements in banking techniques permit in-

creased use of credit. This makes it possible to carry on more trade with a given amount of gold.

3 Gold is used chiefly as a measuring stick, not as a means of exchange, as long as credit is used productively. Under the gold standard, it is no more necessary to transfer gold with every transaction than to buy a new ruler for every measurement. When gold does change hands it is usually to settle balances or to make up deficits. In free markets, as enterprise increases the quantity of trade, it also increases efficiency in trade, so that deficits and unpaid balances decline relatively to the total volume of business.

4 Sharp declines in the price levels under the gold standard are not due to sudden shortages of gold, but to misuse of credit and subsequent repudiation of debts, or to government restrictions on trade and exchange. These conditions cause contraction of credit or prevent use of credit in purchase of goods. For example, the tariff war of 1930-1932, which began with the Hawley-Smoot Tariff Act of the United States in 1930, reduced the saleability and exchange value of goods throughout the world.

5 The surest way to make people want more gold is to prohibit them from having it, or threatening to do so. Inconvertible currency drives gold into hiding or raises its value because it destroys confidence in all other forms of currency.

6 A period of declining prices for staple commodities is likely to be a period of most rapid progress in levels of living for wage earners if the decline arises from increased efficiency in production.

Credit currency may be preferred

For most transactions, credit currency (banknotes or bank checks) is more convenient than gold, and most persons prefer it to gold as long as they believe that it is based on sound investments. Aside from uses in the arts, a person wants gold mainly when he begins to lose confidence in credit, that is, when he fears that the custodians of credit are advancing too much of it for unproductive purposes, so that their gold reserves may be insufficient to meet their possible losses.

In other words, the gold standard restrains credit inflation: no other means of control is so effective for this purpose. At the same time, use of gold in free markets does not prevent expansion of credit sufficient to permit full employment of the economy's productive resources. Under the gold standard, the limits of credit expansion are set by productive capacity, not by the size of the gold reserves.

In free markets, goods generate credit

Prudent persons accumulate reserves of valuable goods, or claims on goods, including reserves of gold and claims on gold. Such reserves improve their credit rating and increase the quantity of credit which they may get or give.

Similarly, where a great many citizens prudently accumulate wealth and build productive capacity, there we find an abundance of credit and buying power as long as the citizens are free to trade with one another and with people of other nations. It is not the great stock of gold which makes the United States the world's greatest reservoir of credit today, but our people's vast output and stocks of exchangeable goods (including gold), which they earn and produce or which persons of other countries entrust to them for safe-keeping.

The basic fallacy of Keynesian theory

This brings us to what is perhaps the basic fallacy of Keynesian thought. The Keynesian economist treats of goods and credit as though they were two quite separate things. He teaches that the output of goods creates a need for credit and currency. He warns that goods may go unsold, forcing down prices and causing unemployment, unless government: (1) adds to the supply of currency as the output of goods increases, and (2) sees to it that those who get the new money spend it promptly.

The classical view, on the other hand, is that goods themselves are the source of all sound credit and sound currency. Let us see what this means.

56

Goods give value to goods

In free markets, every producer may extend credit to the full value of the goods he offers for sale. That is, he may sell all of these goods on credit if he finds customers who can someday supply something he wants in exchange, or who can supply something (goods or claims on goods) which he can trade for what he wants.

In other words, the credit which a producer can give depends on the amount of goods he can get for them in future. This means that the amount of credit available is always potentially equal to the output of goods. It becomes actually equal to output as buyers and sellers agree on prices and enter into contracts.

One problem of maintaining employment and output, therefore, is that of removing obstacles to the making of agreements on the terms of trade, that is, on prices of commodities and services.

Credit vs. credit instruments

Many persons fail to understand the relation between goods and credit because they think of credit only in terms of the paper *instruments* of credit, especially the instruments of bank credit, such as banknotes and bank checks. Of course, when the output of goods and the volume of trade decline, the flow of credit instruments also declines. From this fact it is easy to conclude that the way to increase trade is to increase the supply and rate of circulation of banknotes and bank deposits.

The fallacy of this conclusion should be clear from the evils which ensue when governments try to apply it in practice. But let us consider further the relation between credit and credit instruments.

Credit instruments are the records of credit transactions. They include commercial credit instruments, such as promissory notes, due bills, trade acceptances, I.O.U.s and other evidences of debts.

These paper forms are not credit, but evidences of credit that producers are granting. The real credit consists in the value of goods which sellers give up in return for the buyers' promises to pay later.

Of course, a seller may use a customer's I.O.U. to pay a debt which he himself owes. A private, commercial credit instrument then circulates as currency.

More often, he takes the private credit instrument to a bank which uses it as a basis for granting bank credit (banknotes and bank deposits). He does this because bank credit instruments circulate more easily than commercial instruments.

The bank's business, then, is to substitute its better-known name for the names of nonbanking debtors on the credit instruments used in trade. It accepts commercial instruments at a discount (to pay for its service), and grants bank credit against them. That is, it issues banknotes and permits the drawing of checks to take the place of the commercial credit instruments which it holds as security. Banknotes and bank checks, therefore, are credit instruments, like the nonbank instruments which they replace, except that they are more readily accepted in trade.

Goods pay for goods

Those who buy goods on credit, of course, are debtors. They usually pay their debts with checks on bank deposits and with banknotes which they get by selling goods and services to bank depositors and note holders. In other words, they pay their debts with currency which the banks put into circulation on the basis of the debtors' own original promises-to-pay.

When debtors use credit productively, they create new values which their creditors will pay for. In buying such values, the creditors give the debtors the wherewithal to pay their debts.

The original producers who bring goods to market and sell them on credit, therefore, in effect loan the goods to buyers. These buyers add to the value of the goods, and sell enough of them back to the creditors to settle their debts.

The original buyers keep for themselves any goods left over after paying their debts. They may consume these goods as income or use them to extend credit to other producers. The more productively they use the credit they get, therefore, the more they profit. Thus the productive use of credit increases both goods and credit.

Is saving dangerous?

The Keynesian economist, however, warns that the original sellers may not use all of their credits to buy the new goods as they come to market. He fears they may try to save too much of their credits, for one reason or another. In that case, he says, some debtors may not get enough funds to pay what they owe for goods bought on credit from those who are now holding back their buying power.

One answer to this argument is the fact, shown by Professor Lutz's study of corporate income and outgo (see pages 66-67), that business firms actually spend and invest money about as fast as they get it. In other words, they invest as fast as they save. Apparently they save only in order to invest.

The same is true of much, if not most, saving by individuals. It is saving for specific investment purposes. Some of this saving goes to investment agencies, such as insurance companies and banks. Some of it the owners invest directly in productive equipment or service.

But can banks and other agencies find investment outlets for all possible savings? What is to prevent such savings from running ahead of investments? And, if for some reason savings momentarily exceed investment, will this not reduce total spending and cause the dire results predicted by the Keynesian economists? Will not sales and prices fall, profits decline, and unemployment rise?

Savings increase demand for labor

The answer to these questions is to be found in the nature of the investment demand for funds.

Investment means spending for productive purposes. It means hiring labor and buying materials to produce more goods. The extent of demand for investment funds, therefore, depends on the amount which use of these funds can add to the output of goods. If anyone wants more goods and is able and willing to help produce them, there is a corresponding use and demand for investment funds to hire and equip him for that purpose. The demand for such funds is equal to the desire and ability to earn and consume.

Obviously, if everyone has all of the goods he wants, there will be no demand for more funds to invest in expanding output. Or, if everyone has as much work as he wants to do or can do, there will be no demand for additional investment funds.

Lack of investment demand, therefore, may mean that everyone is fully employed; or it may mean that no one is able and willing to work for the wages he can produce and earn. In either case, no investment can further expand production.

Increased savings, however, would not alter these conditions for the worse. Instead, these savings would have effects precisely opposite to those which the Keynesian economists predict. The pressure of increasing savings seeking investment tends to reduce interest rates. Investors must be satisfied with lower rates of return. This reduces the cost of capital and thus increases the share of the product which employers can offer to wage earners. Therefore, wages rise and the demand for labor increases. Labor that was formerly too inefficient or too high-priced to be employed now becomes employable. Employers can now pay wages sufficient to induce reluctant workers to take jobs.

Inventions increase profits and wages

Inventors and engineers, who increase producers' efficiency, increase rewards for users of capital, both employers and wage earners. The enterprise of every worker looking for a job or trying to do a job better also creates opportunity for investment, because it offers more opportunity to use capital goods and reward investors. Immigration and other means of increasing the labor force increase investment opportunities and demand for savings.

But, although inventions, discoveries, enterprise, and immigration increase the demand for savings, it does not follow that an increase in savings is harmful when these conditions (which Samuelson and other Keynesians call "dynamic factors") are absent.

On the contrary, the increase in savings brings about a division of the product more favorable to wage earners. It increases the demand for labor and the opportunities for employment.

When lower profits mean higher wages

If the increased willingness to save brings down the rates of return on investments, it is because savers are willing to save more than before at former rates or to save as much as before at lower rates. Consequently, the fall in rate of return does not cause them to save less than before or to withdraw their savings. It merely checks the increase and helps bring the rate of saving into equilibrium with the investment demand for funds.

And, even if the increase in savings continues despite the decline in return from investment, the worst that could happen would be that employment opportunities and wages would continue to rise, a result that surely should not be cause for alarm.

Therefore, as long as producers (including wage earners) want work and are willing to share the net output of industry with those who put up the capital, there is a return on investments and a demand for savings. If there is no investment at that rate of return it must be because people prefer to spend their money on consumption goods rather than to save it. In that case, the lack of investment is due to a lack of thrift and savings, not to an oversupply of savings as Keynes contended.

It is the business of entrepreneurs, banks, insurance companies and other investment agencies to ferret out investment opportunities, endorse credits, issue the memoranda we call banknotes or keep the records we call deposit currency, and thus put savings to work.

If there are both idle savings and idle workers, it can only be because of non-economic barriers to production and trade. These barriers may be tariffs, union picket lines, taxes, subsidies to idlers, or government interference with prices and wage rates.

Such restrictions prevent entrepreneurs from arranging terms of exchange and carrying on trade. In others words, the markets are not wholly free.

Inflation robs producers and destroys credit

According to this classical view represented by Anderson, the practical remedy for such a shortage or stagnation of credit is not for government to print money or force an increase in deposit currency, as Keynes proposed. Such a policy does not remove the causes of the stagnation or credit shortage. Instead, it enables those to whom the government gives the new currency to get goods without giving goods in exchange—as a countefeiter does. It robs producers, and it tends to perpetuate the barriers and interferences which are the real cause of the difficulty.

The economic remedy for a shortage of credit is to take away the barriers to the production and exchange of goods, so that producers may create *earned* credit and *earned* credit currency. This policy assures an ample supply of credit and currency. More important, it is the only way for producers to get the goods they want in exchange for their own.

Currency inflation dilutes credit and redistributes it. It finances unproductive expenditures, such as over-expansion of certain industries as compared with others, war costs, private or government extravagance, or purchase of "surpluses" to maintain prices. It creates "debt for dead horses." It encourages unwise speculation, and unproductive investment. It discourages saving. It creates disequilibrium between prices and costs, between the output of capital goods and consumers' goods, and between debts and ability to pay.

The longer such inflation continues, the greater are the vested interests in the uneconomic activities which the new currency finances. These uneconomic activities cause waste of productive capacity. They reduce capital or retard its increase.

All of this increases business uncertainty. Investors know that eventually such credit must be liquidated by burdensome taxes, by cancellation of debts, or by further debasement and revaluation of the currency — or perhaps by a combination of all three. Furthermore, the longer such liquidation is postponed, the greater is the difficulty of making the necessary readjustments when the inflation ends.

Government policies caused inflation, 1913-29

During World War I, as Anderson shows, nearly every government resorted to currency inflation.

This, and the war itself, gave rise to serious economic unbalance throughout the world—as inflation and war always do.

After the war and during the 1920s, governments tried to stave off the depressing effects of this unbalance. They sought to maintain prices and wage rates by policies restricting competition: tariffs, cartels, and unionism. With the help of the Federal Reserve banks of the United States, they continued their deficit financing to support markets by government loans, subsidies, doles, and relief works.

These attempts to maintain unbalanced conditions by restricting trade and expanding the *quantity* of bank credit caused still greater unbalance and further deterioration in the *quality* of credit.

Eventually, the destruction of confidence and credit and the exhaustion of reserves brought about repudiation of obligations and a downward spiral of deflation and depression.

It was not a surplus of savings, therefore, a lack of investment, or an excess of output that brought to an end the boom of the 1920s, Anderson contends but a shortage of new savings and depletion of liquid reserves, due to losses on unsound loans and investments.

Corporations save in order to invest

A statistical study by Professor F. A. Lutz, *Corporate Cash Balances, 1914-43*, bears out Anderson's contention that hoarding of funds was not a cause of the 1929 crash. As far as Lutz's figures show, corporations spend their money about as fast as they get it, and 1928-29 was no exception. Contrary to the assertions of Keynesian economists, these figures indicate that business savings are very closely related to investments.

Corporate "surpluses" are not mainly cash. They are not hoarded, or surplus funds. They are the value of all that the corporation owns, including buildings and machinery, after deducting the amount of liabilities and a certain rather arbitrary figure to represent the stockholders' investment. Business saves to invest, not because it wants to hoard cash or because it does not know what to do with the money; and it spends the money it invests as quickly as any other money it pays out.

"We planned it that way"

One other point Anderson makes clear. The depression of 1930-39 was no ordinary one. It was not merely a "natural reaction," or "period of correction," resulting from previous excesses. It was characterized by more government "planning," throughout the world, than any other in the past 150 years.

This "planning" was supposed to stop the depression and bring back prosperity. It consisted partly of new restrictions on trade to maintain or raise prices. These restraints at once reduced the credit

67

and buying power of producers. Governments also continued deficit spending, which wasted much-needed savings, reduced confidence in currencies and credit, and caused a paralyzing flight of capital from nations with more "planning" to those with less.

In Anderson's view, which he supports with a wealth of factual data, it was these "positive" and "constructive" policies of government which led to the speculative excesses of the 1920s. Further development of the same policies during the subsequent depression prevented the readjustments necessary for recovery. He writes:

> Prior to 1924 we had not regarded it as a Federal Government function to make employment. Employment was a matter for the people themselves to work out. Beginning with the Federal Reserve purchases of Government securities in 1924, we have had Government policy directed increasingly toward making employment. The explanation of the good figure for employment prior to 1924, and of the desperately bad figures for employment which followed 1929, is to be found in precisely this fact. Under an old-fashioned Federal Government, which, in financial matters, was concerned primarily with its own solvency and with the protection of the sound gold dollar, the people themselves solved the problem of employment amazingly well. When the Federal Government took over and undertook to solve the problem for them, grave disasters followed.

> President Roosevelt inherited a terrific volume of unemployment. He did not cure it. The figures for 1933 are worse than the figures for 1932. . . . In only two years of the Democratic New Deal period prior to the outbreak of World War II did the annual average figure for unem-

ployment get below 8,000,000. And in the best of these two years, namely 1937, the figure stood at 6,372,000, which is 12 per cent of the labor force, as compared with 11.2 per cent of the labor force in the year of extreme depression, 1921.

The historical record is damning. The New Deal, viewed as an economic policy designed to promote employment, is condemned by the historical and statistical record.

. . . . The degree of unemployment does not tell the full story. The amount of slack in the industrial situation . . . is also a matter of unused capital and unused technological knowledge. The New Deal policy, as we have seen, had made capital timid in the extreme and had greatly retarded the application of new technology.

. . . .

We came into the period of the second World War with a heavy obsolescence, a large body of unused technological ideas, and a great deal of idle capital,, and, as shown by the foregoing table, with 9,080,000 men unemployed, on the average, in the year 1939.

. . . .

In 1939 we had idle men, idle money, and idle technological ideas on an appalling scale. The war set them to work, but it took the war to do it.[47]

The growing appetite for inflation

The war which put men and machines to work, however, has left the nation with a huge legacy of debt, a crushing tax burden, a depreciated currency, a great dearth of equity (venture) capital, an insatiable appetite for easy money, and an apparatus for inflation that seems irresistible.

Like the war, the current armaments program is giving us "full employment," although less in proportion to the working force than private enterprise usually offered in the much freer markets before 1930, 1924, or 1914. But government spending for armaments, like the spending for war and for prewar relief works, is further distorting economic relationships, adding to debts, liquidating the thrifty, creating new appetites for inflationary borrowing and spending, and depleting the nation's resources.

If we saw any nation but our own following this course, would we be optimistic for its future? We know what such policies have done to other nations. Can our own country escape a similar fate?

The Keynesian economists urge adoption of a "managed currency" and various forms of government intervention in the economic life of their fellow citizens. Their idea is that government should supply an economic wisdom that private enterprise lacks or is unable to use. But even these economists see the uneconomic results of the government intervention which they advocate.

Are these uneconomic results merely unfortunate accidents? Or is there something in the nature of government that must always bring such results from the attempt of governments to manage the economic affairs of the citizens? Can government ever supply private enterprise with an economic wisdom which it would otherwise lack?

IV. Government Is Political

IT IS A FALLACY that government, which is an agency for coercion, can manage the economic affairs of its citizens. This is what the Keynesian economists propose it do in carrying out a "compensatory fiscal and monetary policy." In determining the amount and use of currency, government dictates changes in the opportunities and rewards for the individuals using the currency. This dictation ranges all the way from determining what persons shall get new houses or cars to deciding what persons shall get a chance to play golf or go to school.

Such use of coercion causes moral and intellectual decay of both government and citizenry. Those who apply the coercion become more arrogant and more indifferent to individual rights; the subjects lose incentive and a sense of personal responsibility. Understanding gives way to antagonism, and mutual hostility destroys both the will and the ability to cooperate.

Most persons admit that these are the results in the case of chattel slavery or foreign dictatorships. Why should they not expect the same results to follow every other attempt to get cooperation by use of compulsion?

The one way in which coercion can help to release or increase human energy is in defense against coercion. A defensive use of force neutralizes coercion, leaving peaceful individuals at liberty. In liberty, individuals learn to get what they want by producing it themselves or by getting it from their fellows through voluntary exchange or gift. The result is human progress.

On the other hand, when men use force to take what they want from their fellows or to manage them, they arouse antagonism and destroy cooperation. The results are conflict and insecurity, leading at last to apathy and indolence, stagnation and backwardness.

How bureaucracy may create "planned chaos"

Professor Ludwig von Mises, in his scholarly but readable little books, *Bureaucracy* and *Planned Chaos*, shows perhaps better than any other modern author why government interference with the free market leads to crisis, totalitarianism, and war. Every interventionist measure results in conditions which are even less satisfactory than those which preceded it, as shortages follow price control and black markets follow rationing. Yet, those who favor such intervention usually blame the evil results of their measures on the selfishness, stupidity, or perverseness of individuals. Then they urge more coercion to deal with the new problems. Thus, for example, Samuelson fears that producers may "react perversely" to government spending and subsidies, so that prices and wage rates may rise before full employment has been achieved. In that case, he intimates, the government may have to apply price and wage controls to stop inflation.

The "mixed economy" advocated by the Keynesian economists, therefore, is highly unstable. It moves from crisis to crisis, from one emergency to another, while the currency depreciates, producers are demoralized, demagogy increases, government becomes more despotic, and international friction mounts. This spiral towards totalitarianism and war persists as long as faith in coercion and government planning prevails over a preference for voluntarism and free enterprise. Says Mises:

> Our age has to face great economic troubles. But this is not a crisis of capitalism. It is the crisis of interventionism, of policies designed to improve capitalism. . . .[48]

Government management must be bureaucratic

Why is it that government intervention fails to achieve the results the "planners" hope for?

Mises believes that the answer is to be found in the very nature of government. In *Bureaucracy*, he tries to show that government cannot operate on economic principles because its operations cannot be subjected to the evaluations or checks of economic calculation. By its very nature as a coercive agency, its operations must be circumscribed by rules which restrict the enterprise and discretion of its officials. In other words, it must be bureaucratic, it cannot be businesslike.

In private enterprise, Mises point out, a business owner or the manager of a department may have wide discretion in use of the funds entrusted to him and in the spending of the revenues of his business or department. However, he must show a profit or lose his position; and he earns this profit in voluntary cooperation, competing with every producer in every line. He competes in offering greater economy (*"more for less"*) to customers, investors, and wage earners. A business organization, says Mises, cannot become bureaucratic as long as its operations are guided by the profit motive and are not interfered with by government or private violence.

The profit motive in government, however, results in intolerable tyranny and conflict. This is because government is coercive. Its basic function is using coercion to protect citizens against violence from their fellow citizens or foreign enemies. The restraint of constitution, law, and "red tape" must apply to use of coercion by government, as well as to use of coercion by private citizens. Otherwise government is as dangerous as the criminal or foreign foe. Even in dealing with the suspected or convicted criminal, government officials must observe rules designed to protect suspects and criminals (as well as innocent persons) against unnecessary violence. Laws must say what is a crime and must prescribe the manner of dealing with suspects and criminals.

Totalitarian governments also must operate bureaucratically, because, without rules to guide them, ambitious officials might build the means to declare their independence of the central authority or make war upon it. What authority a totalitarian regime has depends on subjecting subordinates to a rigid control by laws and rules, even though the laws and rules may be quickly changed by orders from the top.

In other words, all governmental departments, whether in a liberal or a totalitarian government, must operate bureaucratically, not according to business principles.

Every government agency uses compulsion

But what of an economic venture like a government-owned power plant? May not that operate according to business principles rather than bureaucratically?

If it is to operate entirely according to business principles, however, why should anyone wish to make it a government project? No one advocates that government step into power production or the railway business or any other business unless he wants to get the operations away from control of business principles in some regard or other.

It is because he wishes at some point to substitute coercion for voluntarism, a bureaucratic rule for profit-making in free markets, that anyone advocates government ownership of anything. He may wish to change the method of getting capital, hoping to get it at lower cost by taxes or by government manipulation of the currency. He may wish to change the method of hiring executives, hoping to get them cheaper and better by political or civil service appointments than by permitting profit-seeking owners to bid for them in open market. In addition, government ownership usually involves use of force to suppress competitors.

Whatever the reason for government ownership, therefore, it has to do with substituting force for the guidance of the free market in directing the operations.

It is this use of force which makes it necessary to substitute bureaucratic rules (red tape) for profit-making enterprise in the management of government undertakings. The central political authority (e.g., the Congress) must specify the field of work, set the limits of expansion, and lay down principles which are to govern the executive in its administrative rule-making. All of this restriction of the profit motive in government is necessary to prevent a government enterprise from undermining the position of the central government and ruling party, or from going beyond a certain point in interfering with the liberty of the citizens.

Government markets cannot be free

Samuelson describes the way in which he thinks a price system might work in a Socialist society. But how could government officials arrive at prices for land and machinery which only "society" may own? If no one owns them, it would be futile and foolish for anyone to offer anything for them. What money one government official may offer another for anything is not determined by business principles, because he is not supposed to be working for profits and he is not judged or rewarded according to the profits he makes.

Of course, in a "mixed economy," the central authorities could not permit an official to set prices that were entirely arbitrary or meaningless. Therefore, they must lay down rules for fixing prices. Without the profit motive to direct them they can only use political criteria for the rules governing price policies. That is, they must lay down price policies that are most pleasing to those who hold political power or to those who can bestow political power. Any other method of pricing would necessarily cost them their jobs.

Precisely the same holds true of government control of interest rates, government control of the value of money, government control of credit policies, or government control of wages and salaries. Once we depart from business criteria set up in free markets, there is left only political criteria established by the methods of winning political control.

Government statistics are political instruments

But what of the statistics of income and employment, savings and investment, price levels and wage rates, that the Keynesian economist proposes to use as criteria for "compensatory fiscal and monetary policy"? What of those mathematical formulas that are supposed to tell us just how much private spending will result from a given increase in government spending? Are not these economic criteria which experts might use to supply some over-all government management along sound economic lines?

Part of the answer to these questions will be found in a later section dealing with the supposed usefulness of the Keynesian approach in business forecasting. At this point, I shall only call attention to the following facts which anyone may verify for himself by a little study of the "parity price" agricultural program of the United States government:

> *First,* the compilation of statistics and the construction of government indexes are themselves political operations, controlled by political considerations and bureaucratic rules. There is no one "right" index of prices, interest rates, rates of profits, or wage rates. There are only various estimates arrived at by bureaucrats subject to poltical pressure and bureaucratic red tape. What

78

index to use is a matter of opinion in every case, and the only way to decide which opinion should determine a government policy is by political and bureaucratic methods and standards. The loyal government official asks, What does the law or executive order tell me to do? Insofar as it is not quite clear or specific, he next asks, What interpretation of this order will be most "politic"? This means, What interpretation will help keep my superiors and me in office?

Second, government policies do not affect people in general, or prices in general, or incomes in general. They affect particular persons at particular moments of time. The choice among which acts of which persons at what times the "planners" are to control must be bureaucratically and politically determined. That is, the "planners" must follow certain rules in deciding what taxes are to be raised or lowered, whose incomes are to be cut or raised, what interest rates are to rise or fall. And these rules must be laid down by other officials who must act politically in order to hold their jobs.

Third, even the arguments and reports of the "experts" in government must have a political slant. They must deal with subjects in which the politician is interested, and they must deal with them in such a way as to help the politician retain and consolidate his authority.

Government planning cannot be economic

If government "planners" hold office for short terms, then their decisions must follow the short-term political changes. If they are appointed for long terms, then they must follow the long-term political trends. But always they must obey the rules which political authorities lay down, and these rules are designed to help keep the ruling party in office. As I pointed out above, government's construction and use of indexes in connection with the "parity-price" program for agriculture in the United States illustrate nicely how politics and bureaucracy decide the issues. From an economic standpoint, the result can be only what Mises calls it—"planned chaos." Government spends millions of dollars to reclaim land for agricultural purposes, and it spends billions more to restrict agricultural output or to buy up the crop "surpluses" for waste and destruction. It gives farmers millions of dollars' worth of advice and aid to increase output, and then it pays them millions more to keep the crops from coming to market.

All government acts are political

Such policies make sense only from a political and bureaucratic standpoint. Bureaucrats are following rules which politicians believe will help them win and hold political office.

Again, therefore, we get back to the question: What is the proper scope of government? Should

80

it determine how much individuals earn, how much they save or invest?

In order to answer these questions, we must realize that government is an agency for coercion, and we should understand how man reacts to coercion or in the absence of coercion.

To say that we can determine the scope of government only by experience, as the Keynesian economists argue, is not enough. Man has already had thousands of years of experience with a great variety of governments and government policies. If a political economist warrants the title "scholar" he should know a good deal about such experience, and he should have derived a set of principles for the use of political force in human affairs. If we have not learned from past experience, why should we expect to learn from future experience?

V. Of Law and Right

Accordingly to one school of thought, government (or "society") creates individual rights, and what government creates it may destroy.

This is the view of those Keynesian economists who want government to adopt a "compensatory fiscal and monetary policy" in order to control the spending and employment, the saving and investing, of individual citizens. This policy calls for taxes, not to raise revenue merely, but to redistribute income, to reduce saving, and to increase consumption, or sometimes to restrict consumption and increase saving. It calls for borrowing, not merely to meet emergency expenses of government, but to expand currency, increase total spending, and raise price levels. It calls for employing labor, not merely to perform the functions of government, but as a means of diluting the currency. All of these activities imply that individuals have no property rights which the government is bound to respect.

In fact, however, the moral rights of self-defense and private property are necessary to human life and to the cooperation we call "society." Man can exist only as he asserts and defends these rights against violation by government or by private persons. He cannot cooperate with his fellows except as they respect these rights. As these rights are invaded, individuals fight or flee from one another, and to that extent society disintegrates and people perish.

For this reason, human rights are prior to society. As government protects these rights, society develops and prospers. Insofar as government infringes on human rights, including property rights, it destroys the cooperation ("society") which supports it.

Majorities may violate individual rights

Some authors recognize that an autocracy may be unjust but appear to believe that a representative government, or democracy, by its very nature, must always be just. As the Keynesian economists, Nordin and Salera say, such a government "means all of us in the community." Is this meant to imply that the lawful acts of an official in a democracy are agreed to by every citizen or that they are for the good of all?

A moment's thought should show the fallacy of such a view. Democracy is not liberty and it does not guarantee liberty. For example, when the citizens "take the law into their own hands" and form a lynching mob, they may carry out the will of all the people except one, the victim, but they do not establish liberty. Similarly, representative institutions and voting may help to limit government and keep it lawful, but they do not necessarily prevent tyranny and injustice. Majorities may vote for government policies that are as tyrannical and collectivistic as those of a monarchy or dictatorship.

Progress starts with one person

Human progress always starts with ideas and acts of individuals who break away from the majority opinion or practice. Such an individual is often highly unpopular. Usually, at first, the majority look on him as dangerous, ridiculous, anti-social, reckless, or foolish. Almost always his actions or plans threaten the security of more people than seem likely to benefit. For this reason, when laws and the constitutions permit, majorities restrict liberty, especially liberty to do better.

Government must, therefore, restrain majorities, as well as individuals and minorities, from interfering with individual liberty. It effects this restraint by law and the constitution. Its officers must enforce the law and loyally uphold the constitution, even in the face of hostile majorities, if liberty is to survive.

To repeat, representative institutions are useful and necessary for good government, but democracy is not freedom and does not guarantee freedom. Majority rule is not "self government" in the sense of individual freedom.

What freedom means

The essential condition for human rights and freedom is non-interference. That is why all great moral codes consist mainly of prohibitions: "Thou shalt *not* kill!" "Thou shalt *not* steal!" "Thou shalt *not* bear false witness!" "Thou shalt *not* covet!" Within the family there is a positive injunction: "Thou shalt honor thy father and thy mother!" But this means, perhaps, that "Thou shalt *not* cast them off to be cared for by someone else when they are old!" Furthermore, it does not give parents a right to enslave their children.

Again, in the Constitution of the United States, especially in the "Bill of Rights," we find that freedom means non-interference. The little word *not* is repeated again and again. The authors of these documents sought to make freedom secure by limiting government, rather than by making it easy for the majority to rule.

Keynesians propose unlimited government

Keynesian economists, along with all other advocates of government "planning," tend to ignore the word NOT in human relations. They put no limit on government authority over the individual and his property except that of political expediency or majority opinion. This is what makes their doctrine essentially coercionist, collectivist, and socialist.

They regard the doctrine of natural rights as a

superstition. They consider it quite proper, for example, that government should seize a citizen's gold, fix its own price for it, and refuse to pay it out again except at its own pleasure and on its own terms. They consider it not in the least reprehensible for a government to announce a change in its paper price for gold, thereby arbitrarily redistributing property between millions of persons doing business in international trade and finance. Could any actions be more arbitrary or show greater indifference to individual rights? Yet, in the Keynesian view, such acts are matters merely of political expediency, no more to be judged moral or immoral than a decision to paint the courthouse gray instead of green.

Keynesians urge redistribution of wealth

Similarly, Keynesians propose that government seize (by taxation) the earnings of the well-to-do and give them to the poor in order to reduce the "propensity to save." They consider this "progressive" or "liberal." Instead, it is a return to the collectivist immorality of our cave-dwelling ancestors.

It was collectivism such as this that kept man for so long in savagery after he had attained reasoning powers. And even after he began to recognize the right of private property, reversions to collectivism again and again cast him back toward barbarism. Taxation that is designed to take from the rich to give to the poor or to discourage thrift is not progressive or liberal but essentially reactionary.

Disregard for property rights

The economists of the Keynes school show the same indifference to property rights in their proposals for manipulating price levels. For example, as mentioned above, Dr. Theodore Morgan suggests that it might be a good thing to have sufficient inflation to raise the general price level by 1 or 2 per cent a year in order to reduce the burden of interest on the national debt and to stimulate business and employment. This would be equivalent to a capital levy of that amount each year on all savings accounts, bonds, and insurance policies, besides an increase of 1 or 2 per cent each year in the tax rate on fixed incomes.

Likewise, these authors propose to redistribute property and income between debtors and creditors by reducing interest rates. Keynes suggested it might be possible and desirable in this way to liquidate the *rentier* class, that is, bondholders and other holders of fixed-income obligations.

In view of this indifference to property rights, one should not be surprised to find a Keynesian economist supporting almost any proposal for increased government authority and interference with individual liberty if he thinks it may help to reduce savings, raise or fix prices and wage rates, reduce interest rates, or "socialize" investment.

Saving requires planning and self-discipline

Conversely, the Keynesian economist has a low regard for the intelligence, responsibility, and integrity of individuals — unless they are in government employ! Since he regards savings for one's old age or other future needs as a dangerous practice, he has little respect (in theory, at least) for what most people regard as essential elements in character, namely, the desire and ability to be responsible for one's own welfare. Saving, according to the Keynesian, is not the result of foresight, planning, and self-control. It is not rational or purposive, he says, but varies with income and is the result of inertia in habits of spending, of outmoded Puritanism, or of neurotic fears.

The fact is that saving is never automatic. At every income level it takes thought, planning, and self-denial. It takes careful discrimination in one's gifts and philanthropies. Persons with these abilities tend to invest their savings wisely and thus to increase their incomes. Such persons are likely also to earn more in wages and salaries than their less farsighted neighbors. For these reasons, it is not (as the Keynesians say) high incomes that cause saving. It is prudence and the "propensity to save" that cause some persons to have high incomes.

The Keynesian cannot admit this. It would make his impressive charts, tables, formulas, and graphs worthless. Once it is granted that his figures deal, not with automatons, but with self-determining and more or less rational individuals, who decide for themselves what they will do, his theories lose all value for purposes of prediction and control.

Little room for self-reliance in the Keynesian ideal

When the Keynesian is brought up against the fact of individual self-determination and variability, therefore, he proposes that government abolish these conditions which upset his calculations! He proposes that government abolish individual freedom and responsibility by means of social-security program.

This program he advocates, not alone on the ground that "we can't let them starve," but on the theory that government can stabilize business by taking over the function of saving. Of course, he is likely to use all of the other social-security arguments to reinforce his own. Consequently, we find Keynesian economists arguing for the social-security program on the ground that people can't save, won't save, and shouldn't try to save.

They are hardly likely, therefore, to impress upon their students that thrift and self-reliance are important virtues in the modern scheme of living.

Keynesism is hostile to private enterprise

Keynesians usually represent profits as resulting from either or both of: (1) a difference between the rate of interest and the "marginal efficiency of capital," (2) monopoly and high-pressure salesmanship. In either case, the recipient of profits is given little or no credit for earning them by useful service.

This Keynesian antipathy or indifference to the qualities developed in free markets arises from the belief that free markets are economically undesirable (e.g., the capital markets) and politically impracticable (e.g., the labor market).

Moreover, as difficulties arise in carrying out their proposals for "socializing" saving and investment, economists of this persuasion usually advocate more restriction of markets rather than less. Thus Dr. Lawrence Klein, for example, favors government price control to prevent inflation that might result from Keynesian "loan expenditures," and he rationalizes this repudiation of freedom of exchange by the contention that "greedy profiteering" was the only liberty infringed by the Office of Price Administration in World War II.[49]

For these reasons, Keynesism is of more than academic interest. It relates to every detail of one's view of social relations. It teaches disregard for property rights. It belittles self-reliance, foresight, and enterprise. It disparages profits. In the name of political expediency, it abandons freedom of trade and free markets.

It is, therefore, antagonistic to the basic economic, moral, and political institutions of private enterprise, or freedom.

90

VI. What of the Future?

SOME PERSONS argue that the Keynesian theory is useful in business forecasting, especially in our present managed-currency world, even though it is unsound as a basis for government policy.

I believe this is a fallacy.

Forecasting is necessary for all business, but stock market gyrations of the past fifty years have centered attention on a kind of forecasting that is of relatively little use, if it is not actually misleading. Business success, large or small, comes mainly from the kind of prevision Henry Ford showed in putting his time and capital into producing a cheap car, or that John Wanamaker had when he introduced the policies of one price and the money-back guarantee into retail trade. Such foresight is not based on quantitative studies of national income, but on qualitative insight into the opinions and feelings, hopes and abilities, of other people.

Keynesian theory not helpful in forecasting

Certainly, any analysis based on notions that savings cause business depression and that debt-creation is the right cure for unemployment is worse than useless as a basis for business planning. Dr. Benjamin Anderson contends that the Keynesian analysis always leads to precisely wrong conclusions. Dr. Rufus Tucker, in an essay entitled, "Mr. Keynes' Theories Considered in the Light of Experience,"[50] some years ago gave numerous illustrations supporting Anderson's view.

The statistician can measure and record certain factors in a situation. His charts and formulas can present a few relationships which held good in the past. Some of these relationships are sufficiently stable that they have to be taken into account in estimating future trends. Statistical studies of the situation in regard to particular industries have considerable value.

But "national-income analysis," even when not based on Keynesian assumptions, is fundamentally defective as a method of business forecasting because it involves a pseudo-scientific, mechanistic view of economics that is wholly unrealistic and dangerously misleading.

What income statistics do not record

What Farmer Jones and Tailor Brown will produce and earn, consume and save, next month or next year, does not mainly depend on what they did last month or last year. Their future efforts depend on decisions which they are making now and which they must make in the future; and the changes in their ideas and behavior are determined mainly by things which the statistician can hardly measure.

Could any national-income figures prior to United States' entry into the Korean War have indicated the business fluctuations which were to follow? True, the period from, say, June to October, 1950, was not typical, but what period *is* typical? Each period in history is like other periods in some ways, but what people think and want are different in every case, therefore what they do is different.

Free markets are not automatic

Success in forecasting depends on what one knows of other people's plans. Knowledge of past and present operations helps in judging capacity to carry out these plans. This is where statistical facts are helpful. But there are always changing human purposes which cannot be tabulated or measured statistically. As Professor Mises says:

> No "automatic" and "anonymous" forces actuate the "mechanism" of the market. The only factors directing the market and determining prices are purposive acts of men. There is no automatism; there are men consciously aiming at ends chosen and deliberately resorting to definite means for the attainment of these ends. There are no mysterious mechanical forces; there is only the will of every individual to satisfy his demand for various goods.[51]

For this reason, none of the quantities, formulas,

93

or relationships used in national-income analysis is fixed or stable, not even the "propensity to save'" or the rate of turnover of funds. This alone makes the "multiplier" worthless for forecasting, not to mention the fallacious assumptions on which it is based.

National-income analysis is supposedly most useful for predicting changes in employment. Yet the increase or decrease in amount of national income per employee added to the working force or subtracted from it varies from year to year by 100 per cent or more. In some years, employment has actually gone up while national income has gone down. In other years, employment fell while total national income rose. In the field for which it was especially designed, therefore, this approach is useless as a tool for forecasting.

National-income figures are useless for forecasting because they cannot record and weigh the infinite variety of conditions which self-determining individuals take into account in building their futures.

This national-income approach, moreover, promotes the notion of the business "cycle." This mechanistic concept has not only been a nuisance in business forecasting, but it has supported the socialistic idea that business fluctuations are the natural and necessary consequences of free markets. Under the influence of this notion, as exemplified in Keynesian theory, governments are more and more pursuing managed-economy policies that are the chief causes of business instability and war.

Government "planning" increases instability

As far as anyone knows, man's conduct is not predetermined, therefore is not predictable in the way that certain natural phenomena, like the weather, may be. Yet, in freedom, human conduct is increasingly rational and cooperative. Therefore, it provides a basis for hopeful planning. This was the truth behind the adage, "Never sell America short!" In voluntary enterprise, success goes to those who bet on increasing opportunities for economic cooperation and who judge more or less correctly what other people want to buy or sell.

In freedom, people cooperate in hope of reward. This means that each person gets the aid of others by offering sufficient inducement to enlist their will — their determination — to do what he wants and expects. Under such conditions, people are more likely to keep their promises and carry out their announced plans than when they are being coerced into something against their will. For this simple reason, business forecasting is much easier in proportion as people are free.

Government intervention, or "management," in economic affairs introduces the element of legalized coercion. Coercion, whether legal or illegal, means abandonment of reason and of appeals to reason as means of getting cooperation. It does not mean merely substituting force for reason. Rather it means suppressing such cooperation as the coercive authority considers undesirable or unnecessary. Thus, for example, taxes suppress the cooperation which private spending would have supported; currency "management" suppresses some kinds of money (e.g., gold) and monetary arrangements in favor of others; government ownership involves prohibitions against competing enterprises or forced levies upon them.

Coercion destroys cooperation

Such coercion and suppression arouses anger or fear, opposition or discouragement, rather·than hope and approval. Whether legal or illegal, it arouses the desire to escape and evade (e.g., "flight of capital"), or to resist and disobey (e.g., "black markets"), rather than to cooperate. It can accomplish its purpose only as it closes avenues of escape and crushes opposition. Up to that point, the victims use their ingenuity to thwart the will of the coercionists. Beyond that point, the victims become hopeless, apathetic, and uncreative. At either stage the results are declining output, trade, and prosperity.

Authors of managed-economy policies are continually coming up against these unpleasant results, which upset their calculations. The remedy which the Keynesian planners urge is currency inflation. But this inflation liquidates the creditor interest which is most opposed to unproductive spending and investment and most opposed to restriction of output which reduces the purchasing power of the currency. At the same time, the currency inflation is used to provide subsidies and support for those who favor unproductive lending and spending and who seek to impose restraints on production and trade. Consequently, larger and larger doses of currency inflation are necessary to overcome the stagnation of trade brought on by government's interventionism, that is, to trick producers into working and exchanging their goods for the depreciating paper promises in the face of rising taxes and increasing restrictions.

Fiat currency nurtures stateism

This use of fiat currency finances the growth of the unproductive, collectivist, and restrictionist State. It liquidates the productive and stabilizing elements. Thus it clears the way for reactionary revolutions, such as the Bolshevik Revolution in Russia, the Fascist Revolution in Italy, the militaristic revolution in Japan, and the Nazi Revolution in Germany. As Keynes himself said before he became a full-fledged "Keynesian":

> *There is no subtler, no surer means of overturning the existing bases of society than to debauch the currency. The process engages all the hidden forces of economic law on the side of destruction, and does it in a manner which not one man in a million is able to diagnose.*[52]

Keynes and his followers, by urging a "managed currency" and "compensatory fiscal policy," have

helped to build in nearly every nation a Franken-
stein monster — a bureaucracy greedy for power,
growing daily more aware of its coercive authority
and more hostile toward individual liberty. To that
bureaucracy, the "new economics" now teaches, we
should give still more authority to tax and borrow,
spend and lend, coerce and restrict, in order that
it may make our jobs and prosperity more safe and
secure.

What grounds are there for thinking that this
abdication of individual right will not mean another
retreat toward individual irresponsibility?

The Keynesian revolution in economics concerns
everyone in the most intimate details of his daily
life. This is not only because of the way the revolution may affect votes and government policies. It
must affect also the attitudes and conduct of individuals toward one another. It must determine their
personalities and characters.

As a man thinks, so he is

The individual's view of man and society determines
the way he feels and acts toward his fellows. His
view of other people's rights determines the way he
discharges his own responsibilities. His view of his
responsibilities determines what he expects from
others and how he tries to get it. A teacher may
profess to deal only with government policy in regard to money and credit, taxes and spending, not

with individual conduct and morality. But how can government control spending and lending, saving and investing, without affecting individual rights and responsibilities in use of money?

In making out their case for government control of private lending, spending, saving, and investing, Keynesian economists must belittle the wisdom with which individuals act when free. They must especially disparage the competence of those private citizens who handle relatively more money than their fellows: the well-to-do and the managers of business enterprise. They imply that American business leaders in the past owed their success to good fortune in being born into a new country with rich, undeveloped resources, or else that they owed it to monopoly, special privilege, near-fraudulent advertising, lucky speculations, and the free labor market which permitted "exploitation" of wage earners.

Is this view of business enterprise likely to make young men more ambitious for business success? Is it likely to encourage honesty, industry, and prudence in those entering upon a business career?

In effect, Keynesian economists teach that Americans are too thrifty, at least much of the time. In order to discourage this thrift they propose that government relieve individuals of their responsibility in providing for the emergencies of life, like old age, unemployment, and sickness. Is that brand of thinking likely to make students eager to become more self-reliant and enterprising?

Keynesian economists may not intend to make their students spendthrift and irresponsible, greedy and covetous; but they provide a rational basis for these attitudes. There can be no question but that their theories imply disparagement of thrift, self-reliance, enterprise, and respect for property rights.

Are these virtues less necessary now than formerly? Some of us, at least, believe that these qualities of character were never so necessary as when the rise of the "Welfare State" is discouraging and destroying them.

"The way to security"

In his latest book, *The Way to Security*, Dr. Henry C. Link points out that human progress and true security come only as individuals develop self-reliance, enterprise, diligence and thrift.

The security which man wants and needs, he says, is first of all spiritual rather than material, a matter of internal feeling rather than external conditions. It depends, not on freedom *from* fear, but on freedom *to* fear, together with freedom to develop the means for overcoming fear. By shielding an individual from life's problems, we keep him from acquiring the ability to solve them. By standing between a man and life's fears, we prevent him from cultivating the power to overcome fear. He writes:

> . . . a government cannot assume responsibility for people's welfare without profoundly affecting their moral

100

fiber. To the extent that government takes care of him, to that extent the adult citizen is deprived of the moral responsibility for himself. . . . The net result is the progressive breakdown in the moral standards of all who participate in the welfare state. The material effect of this breakdown has already been seen in the great depreciation of the dollar. The spiritual and emotional effects are just beginning to receive recognition. . . .[53]

And again:

> If experience and history prove anything, it is that social insecurity may stimulate people to action, to adventure, and so to progress. Social security, on the other hand, lulls people into a state of inaction and stagnation which develops, in time, into a state of jitters.

For this reason, he says, "social security creates the very fears and worries it was intended to cure."[54]

On the other hand, the man who disciplines himself, who denies himself present comforts in order to buy security for his family and himself by his savings and investments, builds spiritual security at the same time as material security. He gains power that gives him a feeling of security *now* at the same time he gains credits that will take care of his needs later.

Furthermore, says Link, the strength of character which individuals develop in liberty is the only possible foundation for the high output, firm contracts, and stable currency necessary for true social security as distinct from the false government security.

And only in liberty do we find growth in those traits of sympathy and understanding that are necessary for genuine philanthropy. The plight of the weak and unfortunate in regimented and collectivist societies is notoriously insecure and wretched.

Coercion decreases security

Increasingly the Keynesian economists are coming to admit the difficulty of preventing currency depreciation under the full-employment policies they advocate. And they know that continuing inflation may destroy security for all. They see also a growing indifference to the public welfare, as, for example, in trade union policies and government's parity price programs for agriculture. They know that this threatens a breakdown of cooperation and that it means less, not more, security for all.

What they cannot admit without repudiating their own program, however, is that the root cause of inflation and of the growing indifference to the public welfare is the deterioration of individual character and morality which Link contends must result from managed-currency policies.

Keynes and his disciples may be right in saying that we cannot reverse the political trend and return to free markets and the gold standard, at least in any foreseeable future.

But if this is so, what is the likelihood that individuals will grow more self-reliant, more far-sighted, more honest and industrious, or more sensitive to the needs of their fellow men? Will Keynesian teachings and policies help develop these qualities? What is the probability that the value of money will become more stable, that governments will become less burdensome and oppressive, or that people will feel more secure? Will a fiat currency and a "compensatory fiscal and monetary policy" bring these conditions about?

Very different from the "note of profound optimism" with which Professor Samuelson concludes his popular textbook, is the view of Professor Link:

> The present scramble for security does not represent the ambition to attain security so much as the nostalgia of a people that wish to retain it! It is not a revival of the spirit of adventure and self-reliance, but the psychology of a nation which has grown soft, a nation which is living on the moral momentum of its past. It does not mean that we are awake to the dangers now threatening our security; rather it means that we are still in a dream world and do not wish to be disturbed. It means, above all, that we have come to think of security almost entirely in terms of material things and have almost wholly lost our understanding of spiritual security.[55]

Not all revolutions bring progress. Ofttimes they are a retreat to a lower level of individual character and social organization. Which are we to expect from the Keynesian revolution in the teaching of economics in American colleges and universities?

We ought to be concerned about the answer. For the revolution aims at the heart of American institutions. It strikes at the roots of individual character.

And it has already proceeded far.

REFERENCES

[1] This study developed out of a series of reviews published by the National Economic Council, Inc., New York, in August and September, 1950.

[2] Seymour Harris (ed.), *The New Economics: Keynes' Influence on Theory and Public Policy* (New York: Alfred A. Knopf, 1947), p. 5.

[3] Harris, *op. cit.*, p. 55.

[4] Paul A. Samuelson, *Economics: An Introductory Analysis*, revised edition (New York: McGraw-Hill Book Co., 1951), p. 261. For a partial list of colleges and universities using this and other Keynesian textbooks see William F. Buckley, Jr., *God and Man at Yale* (Chicago: Henry Regnery Co., 1951), Appendix.

[5] Nordin, J. A., and Virgil Salera, *Elementary Economics* (New York: Prentice-Hall, Inc., 1950), p. 503.

[6] Samuelson, *op. cit.*, pp. 261-62.

[7] Theodore Morgan, *Income and Employment* (New York: Prentice-Hall, Inc., 1947), p. 169.

[8] Samuelson, *op. cit.*, p. 397.

[9] Lawrence Klein, *The Keynesian Revolution* (New York: The Macmillan Co., 1947), pp. 176-77.

[10] Samuelson, *op. cit.*, p. 161.

[11] Lorie Tarshis, *The Elements of Economics* (New York: Houghton Mifflin Co., 1947), p. 512.

[12] *Ibid*, pp. 389-99, 518.

[13] Samuelson, *op. cit.*, p. 417.

[14] Morgan, *op. cit.*, p. 182.

[15] Tarshis, *op. cit.*, p. 391.

[16] Morgan, *op. cit.*, pp. 243-44, 254.

[17] Samuelson, *op. cit.*, p. 685.

[18] Tarshis, *op. cit.*, p. 635. *Cf.* p. 331.

[19] Klein, *op. cit.*, p. 180.

[20] *Ibid.*

[21] Samuelson, *op. cit.*, p. 448.

[22] Tarshis, *op. cit.*, pp. 504-06.

[23] *Ibid*, pp. 534-35.

[24] Klein, *op. cit.*, p. 182.

[25] Samuelson, *op. cit.*, pp. 415-16.

[26] Morgan, *op. cit.*, pp. 242-43.

[27] *Ibid*, p. 175.

[28] Samuelson, *op. cit.*, p. 733.
[29] *Ibid,* p. 734.
[30] *Ibid,* p. 153.
[13] *Ibid,* p. 744.
[32] *Ibid,* pp. 161, 740-42.
[33] Nordin and Salera, *op. cit.,* p. 503.
[34] Samuelson, *op. cit.,* p. 736.
[35] *Ibid.*
[36] *Ibid,* p. 36.
[37] *Ibid,* p. 42.
[38] L. Albert Hahn, *The Economics of Illusion* (New York: Squier Publishing Co., Distributor: New York Institute of Finance, 1949), p. 6.
[39] *Ibid,* pp. 166-67.
[40] Samuelson, *op. cit.,* p. 418.
[41] Hahn, *op. cit.,* p. 169.
[42] *Ibid,* p. 104. *Cf.* pp. 60, 169, 175, 237.
[43] *Ibid,* pp. 36-37, 60, 156 f.
[44] Benjamin M. Anderson, Jr., *Economics and the Public Welfare: Financial and Economic History of the United States, 1914-1946* (New York: D. Van Nostrand Co., 1949), p. 495.
[45] *Ibid,* p. 30-58.
[46] *Ibid,* pp. 317-18.
[47] *Ibid,* pp. 489-94.
[48] Ludwig von Mises, *Planned Chaos* (Irvington-on-Hudson, New York: The Foundation for Ecoonmic Education, 1947), p. 21. *Bureaucracy* (New Haven: Yale University Press, 1944), pp. 111 f.
[49] Klein, *op. cit.,* p. 180.
[05] Rufus S. Tucker, *Mr. Keynes' Theories Considered in the Light of Experience, The Economic Doctrines of John Maynard Keynes* (New York: National Industrial Conference Board, Inc., 1938).
[51] Mises, *Planned Chaos,* p. 29.
[52] John Maynard Keynes, *The Economic Consequences of the Peace* (New York: Harcourt, Brace and Howe, 1920), p. 236.
[53] Henry C. Link, *The Way to Security* (Garden City, New York: Doubleday and Co., 1951), p. 224.
[54] *Ibid,* p. 72.
[55] *Ibid,* p. 74.

The Ludwig von Mises Institute

The Ludwig von Mises Institute, founded in 1982, is the research and educational center of classical liberalism, libertarian political theory, and the Austrian School of economics. Working in the intellectual tradition of Ludwig von Mises (1881-1973) and Murray N. Rothbard (1926-1995), with a vast array of publications, programs, and fellowships, the Mises Institute, with offices in Auburn, Alabama, seeks a radical shift in the intellectual climate as the foundation for a renewal of the free and prosperous commonwealth.

The Ludwig von Mises Institute
518 West Magnolia Avenue
Auburn, Alabama 36832
Mises.org